DREAM

CATCHER

DRE AM
CATCHER

A Passion for People Development

Tinashe Mahupete

≡**IAP**

INFORMATION AGE PUBLISHING, INC.
Charlotte, NC • www.infoagepub.com

Library of Congress Cataloging-in-Publication Data

A CIP record for this book is available from the Library of Congress
http://www.loc.gov

ISBN: 978-1-64113-690-7 (Paperback)
978-1-64113-691-4 (Hardcover)
978-1-64113-692-1 (ebook)

Contents

About Dream Catcher vii

Acknowledgments.. xi

PART **1**

Introduction: *Invest in Your Employees and They Will Invest in You*

1 A Global Dilemma 3

PART **2**

Profiles: *Dream Catcher Deconstructed*

2 Potent Coaches Cultivate Great Talent...17

3 Culture: The Most Important Part of Your Business 23

4 The Worldview of a Winning Coach 35

5 Do I Need to Make Them Happy? A Coaching Pitfall................. 45

PART **3**

Elements: *The Dream Catcher Toolkit*

6 Elements for Coaching 53

7 Think, Talk, and Act Like a Coach 81

PART **4**

Vision. Execute. Sustain.

8 Vision.. 93

9 Elements for a Compelling Vision.............................. 101

10 Execute 119

11 Elements to Execute 129

12 Sustain 145

13 Elements to Sustain 151

14 Conclusion: It never ends! 163

About Dream Catcher

O ver the past two decades, I have had many rich experiences and learned great lessons from QLI, a very unique company based in Omaha, Nebraska, that has become one the United States' premier posthospital centers for brain and spinal cord injury rehabilitation. QLI has worked hard to sustain an employee engagement score in the 90th percentile.[1] Among the many accolades it has received in its over 30 years of existence, the company has been recognized as a "Best Place to Work" in Omaha. This prestigious honor is awarded after a rigorous process administered by the Greater Omaha Chamber of Commerce and Baird Holm LLP to companies with the best work cultures.[2] In a city that is home to world-renowned and significant economic-driving employers such as TD Ameritrade, Nebraska Medicine, Union Pacific Railroad, and Berkshire Hathaway, it is an amazing feat for QLI to have won on all eight occasions that it has entered. It was in this amazing workplace that I was able to cultivate, curate, and now share the Dream Catcher coaching program.

There are numerous depressing accounts of people lying on their deathbeds and reflecting back on life wishing that they had done certain things differently; perhaps taken particular chances or made bolder decisions. They have regrets that start with the words, "I wish I had . . ."

Businesses do the same. The great ones sit with their team members and ask what they can do to improve, to produce and deliver better products and services and encourage their people to dream big. But many, despite discussing all of what could be, don't take the necessary steps to lead their companies to where they desire. This book gives you the opportunity to take these steps, to understand where your business and its people are now, and how to get to where you want to be. It serves as a guide to pursue the dreams and vision for your organization and its members.

Dream Catcher derives its methods from neuroscience and the idea of neuroplasticity—the brain's ability to change and, in effect, to learn.[3] These methods debunk the myth that you can't teach old dogs new tricks. No one—and no business—has a ceiling for growth that they cannot rise above. These methods have been proven in fields such as rehabilitation where patients with traumatic brain injuries have been able to learn or re-learn effectively. *Dream Catcher* provides users with positive, habit-forming techniques that can be customized and applied to any industry. The outcomes result in both productive lives and successful businesses.

There is simplicity to the Dream Catcher program. Drawing on a wealth of examples and case studies, it provides the reader with real-world experience that they can apply to their specific environment. It is designed in a chronological three-pronged and trademarked process centered on core principles that I call *Elements*. These Elements act as a toolkit to help the coach guide each client through the program. This book walks the reader through the process and enables them to apply the Elements to each stage of the program to help their clients acquire new skill sets. The three stages involve the coach guiding the client through the process of creating a compelling *Vision*, helping their clients to *Execute* by taking steps to realize that vision, and finally, utilizing the Elements so that each client develops lifelong habits they can *Sustain*. Together, I abbreviate these three stages as VES.

The book is logically organized into four main sections as follows:

Part 1: Introduction

This section examines the value of coaching for businesses. Globally, companies have to deal with the issue of an escalation in their labor costs. Those that see human beings solely as an expense have and will continue to have problems as they experience low returns and ultimately, extinction. Dream Catcher, as a people-focused coaching program, focuses on maximizing the value of employees and thereby increasing the health and, ultimately, the profitability of organizations. It is a proven modality that organizations can utilize to help their employees, and, in turn, help their businesses develop. The reader is given an overview of the simple yet structured, potent, and effective framework of the Dream Catcher coaching program. The section uncovers how organizations can guide their employees to make better decisions about themselves and their role within their companies. The reader assumes the role of a coach and begins to acquire knowledge that will help them to understand and solve the problems that hinder employees' (referred to as "clients" throughout the book) skill acquisition and gap closure.

Part 2: Profiles

This section of *Dream Catcher* outlines the three main factors that will ensure the success of the scalable and customizable coaching program.

The first factor is the organization and its culture. The reader is provided with an understanding of the optimal organizational environment in which Dream Catcher will be successful. If the prevailing conditions are not conducive, the reader receives detailed guidance on how to develop the right culture within the organization.

The second factor is the inherent required qualities of the Dream Catcher coach. This is briefly touched on here as it is explored in more depth later. Finally, the profile of the ideal Dream Catcher client is considered. By focusing on these three factors (organization, coach, and client), the path to a successful coaching program is established. It is in this section that the reader develops a deeper understanding about the leadership modality of coaching and how it differs from mentoring—a distinction that confuses many.

Througout the book, I outline the responsibilities of a Dream Catcher coach in relation to their client. Dream Catcher has a significant emphasis on an internal locus of control.[4]

This vital ending to the section cautions the coach to not view themselves as being accountable for their client's happiness. Altruism is good. Too much altruism is unhelpful in the coaching process.

Part 3: Elements: The Dream Catcher Toolkit

The Dream Catcher coaching model is designed to help coaches guide their clients through a process whereby they create a vision, formulate a plan, execute steps and apply the necessary practice towards attaining their vision, and establish new positive habits that the they can sustain over time. To achieve all of this requires necessary tools, which I call Elements. The coach gets an in-depth understanding of what each of these six Elements are and, by using recent research and case study examples, why each of them are important. The section provides a detailed guide on how the Elements should be applied to coaching and how to facilitate their acquisition if the client does not already have them as part of their life.

Finally, this section of the book provides the prospective coach with some specific skills that will help them interact with clients who behave in particular ways. The coach will now have started to develop some of the effective skills and the required mindset.

Part 4: VES: Vision. Execute. Sustain.

This part of the book is designed to help the coach understand what it means for their client to create a Compelling Vision, why it is important in the coaching process, and how to facilitate the process with a client while also creating a plan for them to execute. The coach is guided through a series of actionable steps that will enable their clients to execute their vision.

Finally, this section is designed to help the coach attain the necessary understanding of how to help their client build sustainable habits.

Dream Catcher's VES process helps the prospective coach understand how to utilize the Elements as a toolkit for each part of the VES process. The coach learns about potential obstacles or challenges that will likely arise and how to overcome them.

The whole process is then wrapped up with a recap of the life cycle of the Dream Catcher experience. It summarizes aspects that were introduced in earlier chapters that are important for the coach to remember. As with a user manual, help and advice is provided to the coach regarding issues or problems that may require troubleshooting.

Notes

1. Christen, C. (2018, May 06). Best places to work survey identifies the cream of the crop in employees' eyes. *Omaha World-Heralder.* Retrieved from https://www .omaha.com/best-places-to-work-survey-identifies-cream-of-crop-in/article _9f511398-4560-5c3d-a4e5-392cf8ad34b7.html
2. Greater Omaha Chamber. (n.d.). Retrieved September 01, 2018, from https:// www.omahachamber.org/
3. Rock, D., & Page, L. J. (2009). Coaching with the brain in mind: Foundations for practice. Hoboken, NJ: Wiley.
4. Spector, P. E. (1988). Development of the work locus of control scale. *Journal of Occupational Psychology, 61*(4), 335–340.

Acknowledgments

I would have to write a whole separate book in order for me to aptly acknowledge every person who has helped this book become a reality. Regardless, thank you to everyone I have had a conversation with regarding life. Every interaction we have had has been meaningful and I cannot exclude any of that from the experiences that shaped the outcome of this enterprise.

I did not set out with the intent of authoring this book or any book for that matter. If I had known earlier how challenging and difficult of a task it was, I doubt I would have mustered the courage to begin the process. It began with a mentor, Glenn Van Ekernen, encouraging me to write down my thoughts. Thank you Glenn for helping to initiate this very fulfilling endeavor. None of this would have been possible without my friend and wife, Sabrina. You are the amazing and critical editor of my life and a wonderful encourager. Thanks for holding down the fort at home and being there with Dominic and Jada when I was busy with this challenging labor of love.

I'm eternally grateful to Patricia Kearns. You gave me the space and liberty for *Dream Catcher* to become what it is. You provided latitude to apply the principles and fine-tune them at QLI. Thank you Team QLI for being the best place to incubate and hatch meaningful, innovative, and life-changing concepts. Dream Catcher is just one of the many amazing things conceived there.

Mom, you have been the best coach for me. Thanks for teaching me discipline, manners, respect, and love. Thank you also for helping me to

Dream Catcher, pages xi–xiv
Copyright © 2019 by Information Age Publishing

see who I am in the world: never accepting the role of a second-class citizen or having a victim mentality.

To all the Dream Catcher coaches at QLI, you were the first who helped clarify the process and define what worked and what to throw out. Thanks for your patience, working through my disorganized thoughts, and critiquing my initial drafts. Dr. Hoogeveen and Mindset LLC; thank you for all of the pearls of wisdom about leadership that you have helped ingrain in me and in my life. The amazing foundation that you established at QLI has led to true excellence in terms of organizational culture.

Kristopher Kluver guided me in helping to clarify the direction of this book. Your free consultation and direction is something that I will be forever indebted for.

The process of writing is quite easy if you surround yourself with people willing to endorse every thought that you have. Thanks to Jon Pearson for helping sharpen the process. And thank you to Steve Kerschke for the intellectual conflict. I am forever indebted to many who called me out when I didn't have the science to back the theory.

To all that I have coached along the way, thanks for your patience as we worked through what was initially a very gray and murky process. You helped bring out the best in me. More especially, I'd like to thank Kristin Slater. You will be forever remembered as the person who challenged me and taught me who the ideal Dream Catcher was. I only hope and pray that I get to work with more people like you.

Carsten Froehlich, I can never thank you enough for your dedicated approach to the final edits. Thank you for spending late nights and going into the wee hours of the morning perusing through this book. You were dedicated to making sure it is the best effort I can deliver. Your editing prowess is second to none.

Thanks a million to John Stuart for your help in getting this book in front of publishing houses and helping to guide me in this unknown voyage. You have amazing insight into the publishing process, which I knew nothing about. I think that I now understand about 5% of how it works! Thank you for landing me a great publishing deal. You are diligent and deliver what you promise.

To everyone at Information Age Publishing, thank you for believing in me and the aims of this book—developing people, businesses, and communities. I anticipate that great things will come of this.

All I had were words written down on paper until I met Anthony Banks. Anthony, thank you very much. Your ability to listen and your drive to bring out the best by telling stories through art is unrivaled. You are not only skilled you are competitive and want only the best for everything that you touch. Thank you very much for helping visualize the Dream Catcher story through your amazing illustrations.

To my brother, Ebenezer Mahupete, you have read every article and scrap of text that I have sent your way. Thanks for sharing the dream with me. Thanks also to the rest of the Mahupete clan who have always pushed each other to realize our best selves: Rudolph, Rumbie, Ruth, and Rodrick. I love you guys. Finally, thanks to my dad for teaching me the tough lessons I had to learn and the value of working hard. I know you're smiling down on us all (RIP).

There are so many people I have likely forgotten, but if I have not mentioned your name, rest assured that all of you have been instrumental in helping *Dream Catcher* come to life.

Aileen Warren
Alicia Elson
Alyssa Conn
Amy Johnson
Bobby Gill
Bryan Findell
Chris Gille
Chris Schlagenhauff
Chris Tointon
Daniel Dzikiti
Ellie Newman
Erin Lassen
Farhan Khan
Jay Wilkinson
Jeremy Stoll

Joni Wheeler
Kinyarie Dethloff
Kristin Carbullido
Kristin Custer
Dr. Kudzai Chikwava
Mike Joyce
Mindset LLC
QLI
Roni Welch
Sam Nigro
Tariro Chinwadzimba
Taylor Kerschke
Todd Foje
Trev Alberts

Thank you all for sharing your passion for developing people.

PART 1

Introduction

$$1$$

A Global Dilemma

Zimbabwe. My motherland. I will always love the beautiful place that I called home when growing up. But like any other place, it also had some shortcomings. Rhodesia was renamed Zimbabwe after becoming independent from the United Kingdom in 1980. Since then, it had the same man, Robert Mugabe, as its president for almost four decades until his resignation in 2017. The challenges Zimbabwe endured have not improved under different leadership. The saga continues. There has been widespread corruption and a series of economic crises brought the nation to its knees, leaving a mere 10% of its citizens formally employed.[1] These are some of the reasons that led me, along with millions of other Zimbabweans, to leave the only home we had ever known.

This is why I came to America to study. As an international student my tuition fees were double those of a U.S. enrollee and I had to work to support myself. I felt very fortunate that a position at QLI was one of the very first jobs that I found.[2] Even as an entry-level employee, I was happy and satisfied with the working environment. I started to compare my experiences at the company with those that I had in Zimbabwe and found them to be vastly superior to the work culture that I had left behind. This led me to make some general-izations, such as: "Wow, America is a wonderful place to work."

However, my first impression—that QLI represented the typical Ameri-can work culture—proved to be rather optimistic. Few companies, either then or today, placed much worth on the well-being and developmental potential of their employees. I met a host of different people from many different professions and backgrounds in my first couple of years in the United States and my experiences, along with their feedback, helped me to understand some important truths about work culture.

Since 2000, through my experiences with employers and employees across the country, both large and small, I have come to agree with many of the conclusions reported by researchers over the years.

1. Terrible work culture is not a Zimbabwean thing. It is a global issue that plagues many businesses around the world.
2. A poor work culture will affect the employees of any company nega-tively and in turn the business will also suffer.
3. Even businesses with the perfect product or service, the best sales and marketing team, and ample capital will fail to be as great as they desire to be if they do not foster a positive work culture.

The Slow Death of Your Company

"Rising labor costs are evident across almost all major industries," accord-ing to economist Sarah House in a 2018 report.[3] Executives and investors around the globe agree that payroll is among the highest operating ex-penses their businesses face. Depending on the industry, this expense can easily amount to 25–40% of an organization's budget. According to some of the best global research, 70% of these labor costs are spent on people who aren't going to be of any assistance in helping their organizations meet whatever their definition of success is.[4]

Gallup argues that businesses are failing because the majority of their workforce isn't growing or performing to their fullest potential.[5] Over half are disinterested in their company despite showing up for work every day. Almost one out of every five employees are so detached that they are actu-ally working *against* their company's mission, are frequently absent, impact the rest of their team members adversely, and are actively driving customers *away* from their company.

Of course, not every successful business model needs a big labor force. Some successful businesses are run by self-employed "solopreneurs" and use freelancers. Low payroll doesn't necessarily mean low revenue. I have studied a few companies run by solopreneurs and other ventures with very few employees. These people have managed to create amazing companies with millions of dollars of revenue. Allen Walton's Spy Guy security company and The Babysitting Company started by Rachel Charlupski are just two of many such examples.[6,7] The very humble Spanx founder, Sara Blakely, is a billionaire who has benefitted from having very low payroll expenses, especially in the earlier years of her company.[8] This is a critical factor to consider if you're an entrepreneur looking to establish a business.

However, for the rest of the business world, it is a fact that they will have to address the complex issues of hiring people who will be engaged with the mission and aims of the company. Many companies profess to know about the importance of employee engagement and yet only a few actually know how to make it happen. Employees routinely report that their company does not value their voices or that their organization doesn't care to listen or empower them. Yet, as Gallup has identified, successful companies select managers based on their talent for supporting, positioning, empowering, and engaging their staff.[9] Moreover, many companies spend huge sums on coaching their employees. So, why does the problem of employee disengagement persist? It is time for a paradigm shift in the way business is conducted.

People: Expense or Investment?

"Labor," as a word on a business financial statement, is simply a cost that must be monitored and managed meticulously in order to protect profitability. Organizations that only see their people in this way will soon find that their workforce has become toxic.

In meeting with executives, managers, and supervisors, I have asked if the world of work would be different if all organizations treated their employees more like investments rather than costs. The answer has been a resounding, "Yes!"

> "IT IS ONE OF THE MOST BEAUTIFUL COMPENSATIONS IN THIS LIFE THAT NO MAN CAN SINCERELY TRY TO HELP ANOTHER WITHOUT HELPING HIMSELF."
>
> —Ralph Waldo Emerson

We need to treat people as importantly as businesses treat their investments, with the expectation of future gains. Globally, there are exceptional companies who see employees as vital investments and have become magnets, attracting the very best talent.[10] Similarly, organizations that have worked with Dream Catcher LLC have noted very positive results in terms of staff engagement. Many other companies pay lip service to the idea of investing in people yet have not taken the necessary steps to put plans into action because of the time, money, and effort required to make this happen. These organizations have effectively resolved to allow their companies, characterized by 70% plus disengagement rates, to decay and slowly die.[11] It doesn't have to be this way.

Dream Catcher is written for anyone who is in, or wants to be in, a role to invest in, develop, and positively influence the people you work with. In effect, you will be a people "coach" and for that reason I will refer to you, the reader, as "coach" throughout. After you read this book, you will be well on your way to understanding the Dream Catcher program and the role of a coach in actualizing it. As you assume this role, I will refer to the people that you are developing—likely employees in your organization—as your "clients." By reading this book, you will have taken a step that many of today's business leaders aren't bold enough to take.

The Dream Catcher process is designed to arm you with tools to improve people. But it is not only helpful for the success of your team members and business. I believe that you will find that it is also an investment in you.

Businesses *are* people. The growth and success of a business must be mirrored by the growth of its people. The growth of people must in turn come through the development and advancement of the environment they are a part of, at work and in life.

I, along with others who have been using the Dream Catcher program, have derived great satisfaction from seeing the results borne out of investing in people and organizations. When you are done with this book, you will be in a hurry to coach others. I ask you to please remember something important when you are in the midst of helping such people and your organization grow. Take a little time out to pause and enjoy the impact that you have. Smile and enjoy the realization that *you* are making an impact. You will have the privilege and honor of being a part of something special in your organization, community, and especially, in someone else's life.

> "THE PERSON BORN WITH A TALENT THEY ARE MEANT TO USE WILL FIND THEIR GREATEST HAPPINESS IN USING IT."
>
> —Johann Wolfgang von Goethe

Invest in your employees and they will invest in your mission!

Discover Purpose the Dream Catcher Way

We are all born with a purpose! Everyone has a gift. It's like the old story I was told as a child, and that I have retold to my children and others who can put up with my animal analogies.

The Eagle and the Hen

A baby eagle became orphaned and a farmer picked him up off the ground. The farmer took the baby eagle and placed it with his chickens.

The baby eagle learned to imitate the chickens. He would scratch the ground like them, finding and eating seeds, grit, little insects, and worms. He would feed just like the other chickens. It was quite clear that he grew up thinking he was a chicken.

Then, one day, an eagle flew over the barnyard. The eagle looked up and wondered, "What kind of animal is that? How graceful, powerful, and free it is." Then, he asked another chicken, "What is that?" The chicken replied, "Oh, that's an eagle. We chickens aren't able to fly like that."

The eagle went back to scratching the ground. He continued to behave like the chicken he thought he was. Finally he died, never knowing the grand life that could have been his.

Yes, I end it like that, even when I tell it to my children. Suddenly. No "happily ever after."

Just like the self-domesticated eagle, some people never discover their own true purpose and their dream. Sometimes, they simply forget what it was. They follow their peers and try to become like them. It doesn't take much for them to quickly forget and wastefully discard their own unique self. Everyone knows such a person. If you are that person, don't wait until it is too late to think back at what could have been. Don't wait until after the eulogies have been read and those that loved you recall how life could have been different. I have seen that with so many people close to me. It pains me to imagine how much they regretted as they said goodbye to this life.

Dream Catcher identifies the purpose that all people have and empowers you to dig deep, and find and appreciate your strengths. By doing so it enables you to discover your true self and be able to effectively coach talent within your workplace.

Live your purpose: Dream. Dare. Do!

Happier in the Dungeon

Jeremy is one of those well-read individuals whose extensive knowledge about a variety of subjects is impressive. I worked with him at QLI several years ago and I remember how full he was of youthful curiosity, consistently questioning the status quo. On each forearm, Jeremy has a cogwheel tattooed in black ink. I never asked what they represented, but they suited his personality well—a guy that always has his gears turning.

Jeremy left QLI to pursue other adventures in life. Later, I ran into him at an after-party for a local conference I was attending. He had just completed code school and was looking for a job. It was tough finding one because he had no experience and the situation was challenging because he had recently married, purchased a home, and had a little boy. Coincidentally, I knew someone who owned a software development company who was at the party and I made a brief introduction. A few weeks later, Jeremy let me know that he would be visiting for an interview. Shortly afterwards he told me he had done well enough to get a job there.

Jeremy and I stayed in touch as he was also moonlighting while working for his new employer. He did some freelance work and helped build the website, www.idreamidare.com, which is a part of the Dream Catcher coaching program. Jeremy shared some details about his new job. No one micromanaged him, he had autonomy, and the company was driven to make sure that its employees saw themselves as an integral part of the organizational family. He worked with experienced developers who had come from other organizations and felt liberated by not having project managers breathing down their necks. For all of them, this environment was a breath of fresh air. The company kept a couple of beers on tap and at the end of a long day, they could hang out, playing ping pong and other games around the spacious, well-lit office. For a year, Jeremy worked hard and kept pushing himself to learn. His boss, also the owner of the company, sat in close proximity and so they communicated often.

Then, Jeremy quit!

I was very surprised. Jeremy told me that he would regularly ask his boss what he could do to push himself more but was always told that he was doing fine. His paycheck reflected that, and the bonuses showed that he was appreciated. But Jeremy kept asking for a new challenge, a push. He was asking to grow. Jeremy told me: "It was a no news is good news type of culture."

When he left, he told his boss that he was moving on because he didn't feel sufficiently challenged. His boss didn't quite understand. The work he was giving Jeremy was a challenge in itself. What was he truly looking for?

When Jeremy told me about where he was now going to work, I had many questions. He was leaving a company with such an apparently great culture, fun environment, and good pay to somewhere quite the opposite. He was going to work in the windowless basement of a 1920s building for Omaha Public Schools.[12] Since his move, I have asked him about how he has found the change of environment. His response? "I love it." Jeremy went on to elaborate how much he is challenged in his new role. He shared how much he felt like the team and the work that they were doing stretched him beyond what he expected. They helped him by clearly letting him know how he was performing and what they expected from him in his role.

Jeremy's story has helped me understand a few things about what companies are doing to put a Band-Aid on the issue of employee disengagement. No matter how cool or relaxed the environment appears to be, regardless of how many ping pong tables and craft beers people get to drink at the end of the work day; people desire something more. The "No news is good news" culture may be attractive for some employees, but it is not going to help you to retain your very best team members. Moreover, not investing in your team members' development is demotivating and disengaging your employees. It may not be as clear as losing a big account, but if you don't think losing good team members like Jeremy is a big deal, your team and your business is heading downhill. Take a good look at your organization. Do you have people like Jeremy who would rather opt for the dark windowless basement over the beanbags and ping pong tables so that they can be challenged as individuals and team members?

Dream Catcher: It's For You!

Dream Catcher is for people like Jeremy's boss who had no clue why Jeremy was leaving. I have clients in a few different industries. One of them is a young and ambitious dentist, Dr. Chikwava, who at times just goes by the name Dr. C. The dentist owns a practice called Beautiful Smiles by Design, which is located in Dalton, Georgia. The difference between Dr. C. and Jeremy's boss is awareness.

"I went to school to be a dentist," Dr. C. told me when we chatted about the challenges he was facing in his business. "They didn't teach me how to lead, manage, and coach people." He was pretty clear about the challenges he faced and the personnel issues that gave him trouble. I enjoyed working with Dr. C. because of his openness, determination, and hard work. He was always looking at new ways in which his practice could be cutting-edge. Not only did he approach his business in this way—it was also very much the case in his personal life. Seeing the ratings and reviews of his practice, coupled with how busy his office is, it's no wonder that he has achieved the reputation that he has. Dr. C. has used Dream Catcher's program and applied it to his practice in order to grow, both as a business leader and a coach who invests in developing his team members. So confident has he become in his leadership and coaching prowess that in 2018 he opened another practice in Calhoun, the next town over from Dalton. When I attended the grand opening, his team members, so proud of a business that has invested in them, volunteered to host the event and were not slightly deterred by the rains that day.

Dream Catcher is for anyone in any industry who believes in the potential of others and wants to invest their time in learning how to help them reach it.

Executives, managers, and supervisors have appreciated learning the skills that it takes and the value that is derived from getting to know people who start out as mere employees and end up feeling a sense of belonging to the company. They become *real* team members. Relationships deepen as the team members feel that their company is invested and interested in them. A sense of reciprocity is created and employees develop a deeper desire to want to know about and contribute more to their organization and its mission.

What is Coaching?

Coaching is different from other human and social capital development tools such as counseling and mentoring. A great inspiration of mine in the realm of coaching is the American surgeon, writer, and public health researcher, Atul Gawande. Not only is Dr. Gawande a great presenter, skilled at synthesizing complex theory on coaching, he is as capable and credible as a coach as he is open to being a recipient of good coaching. Gawande wrote an article for *The New Yorker* in October 2011 that has inspired and mobilized the greatest and most forward thinking minds in the field of medicine. Entitled, "Personal Best," it was in many ways revolutionary.[13] From a personal perspective Gawande explains how, after almost a decade and over two thousand operations as a specialist in endocrine surgery, he felt he was rather comfortable with considering himself a good surgeon. His competence, when correlated to his results on the operating table, was impeccable. After all, don't people typically see medical success as making it out of a risky surgical procedure both alive and in better shape than before the procedure?

If it ain't broken, don't fix it! Right? Wrong!

Not through any calamity on the operating table, he decided to look at what "fixing it" really meant. The good doctor, famous for the successful outcomes of his patients, started looking at the world differently. He began studying elite performers in a number of fields. Gawande focused on the tennis great Rafael Nadal, who had already won several Grand Slam events. As he watched the Spaniard from Mallorca playing on the Tennis Channel, he noticed how, during the match, the camera often focused on his coach. Gawande wrote, "The camera flashed to his coach, and this obviously struck me as interesting: even Rafael Nadal has a coach, as does nearly every elite tennis player in the world. Professional athletes use coaches to make sure they are as good as they can be."

Curiosity fueled the surgeon, who started noticing that coaching wasn't something solely used by athletes who sought expert performance, it was also common for concert violinists, singers, and even teachers. His quest led him to the conclusion and belief that he too could improve his already exceptional skills as a surgeon. Gawande sought out the services of a coach and they embarked on a plan to make the already great surgeon, better.

As a result of this process, he observed, "Coaching done well may be the most effective intervention designed for human performance. Yet the allegiance of coaches is to the people they work with; their success depends on it. And the existence of a coach requires an acknowledgment that even expert practitioners have significant room for improvement." Coaching is therefore certainly about bringing out one's personal best, but more importantly it is about acquiring the skills for expert performance.

The qualities of the coach are paramount to the success of any coaching effort. The Dream Catcher method is centered on coaching the coaches so that they are equipped with the necessary skills to help others reach expert performance using a tried and proven process and effectively applying its methods.

What Specific Situations is Dream Catcher Useful For?

This is not a one-size-fits-all program. It is a tool kit for developing coaches using a patented science-backed method called Dream Catcher®.

Dream Catcher is a program that is designed to assist coaches who will guide individuals and organizations to conquer challenges by becoming proficient in the art and science of mastering the use of *Elements*, which clients will then use to create a Compelling *Vision* and become big *Dreamers*. The program is designed to then help these big dreamers identify where they currently are in relation to their Compelling Visions. For clients, this realization can be intimidating, as there is usually great distance—what we refer to as "The Gap"—between the "now" and the "Compelling Vision." Dream Catcher doesn't disregard this. Instead, the program takes a tried, proven and evidence-based approach to effectively closing "The Gap." Effective gap closure means that clients learn how to successfully attain skills in specific areas or disciplines and are then also able to apply the same methods to other areas of their work and life. Dream Catcher is unlike other coaching programs that, while geared to results, aim only for the short-term. Completing this program empowers coaches to ensure that their clients will learn how to sustain new habits over the long-term.

Clients are not restricted by age, gender, or other superficial attributes. If they fit the profile (as discussed in the next chapter), they are candidates. This program is geared to building a wealth of individuals who will develop the skills needed to help others become expert achievers and attain their dreams. Dream Catcher methods have been applied to clients who had specific goals and have successfully:

- built soft skills (e.g., leadership, negotiation, relationship building, conflict resolution, public speaking, time management)
- learned hard skills (e.g., writing, studying, job speed, user programs)
- became more confident in work and in life
- gained clarity and control over their future
- developed their careers
- stepped outside of their comfort zones
- cleared obstacles and hurdles they identified as problematic in their lives
- discovered their learning style
- increased their performance
- become experts in a chosen area

Using the Dream Catcher principles and process has changed the lives of many people in organizations. In turn, this has invariably shaped how people in those organizations have made a new commitment to its mission and success.

SUMMARY

Your mission's success is dependent on you investing in your employees.

Are your team members engaged? If they aren't, your organization is at risk of failing.

Dream Catcher is a tool that helps to create real returns for your organization on your investments in developing its people.

A sense of purpose for your team members is vital for their engagement.

Kill the "no news is good news" approach to running your organization.

Dream Catcher leads to bringing out the best in people.

If you want expert level performance in your organization, use the Dream Catcher program.

Dream Catcher methods result in:

- empowered team members
- trust in senior leadership
- pride
- engaged team members
- succession planning
- buy-in for the organizational mission

Notes

1. Reality Check Team. (2017, December 03). Are 90% of Zimbabweans unemployed? *BBC News.* Retrieved August 31, 2018 from https://www.bbc.com/news/business-42116932
2. The QLI Difference. (n.d.). Retrieved September 01, 2018 from https://www.qliomaha.com/
3. House, S., & Vaisey, A. (n.d.). Economics from Wells Fargo. *SBC Magazine.* Retrieved from http://digital.sbcmag.info/publication/?i=485536&article_id=3047265&view=articleBrowser&ver=html5#{"issue_id":485536,"view":"articleBrowser","article_id":"3047265"}
4. Gallup. (n.d.). State of the American workplace. Retrieved from https://news.gallup.com/reports/178514/state-american-workplace.aspx

5. Allen, J., & McCarthy, M. (2017). *How to engage, involve, and motivate employees: Building a culture of lean leadership and two-way communication.* New York, NY: Productivity Press.

6. https://www.spyguy.com/

7. http://thebabysittingcompany.com/bio/

8. Sara Blakely Biography. (2016, March 14). Retrieved from https://www.biography .com/people/sara-blakely-031416

9. Sorenson, S., & Garman, K. (2013, June 11). How to tackle U.S. employees' stag- nating engagement. *Gallup: Business Journal.* Retrieved from https://news.gallup .com/businessjournal/162953/tackle-employees-stagnating-engagement .aspx?g_source=link_newsv9&g_campaign=item_167975&g_medium=copy

10. Best Small and Medium Workplaces in Europe. (n.d.). Retrieved from http:// www.greatplacetowork.net/best-companies/best-workplaces-in-europe/best -small-and-medium-workplaces-in-europe

11. Gallup. (n.d.). State of the American workplace. Retrieved from https://news .gallup.com/reports/178514/state-american-workplace.aspx%20State%20 of%20the%20Global%20Workplace_Gallup%20Report.pdf

PART 2

Profiles

Dream Catcher Deconstructed

2

Potent Coaches Cultivate Great Talent

Cinnamon: The "Cure All"

My wife, Sabrina, made an important life decision some years ago. She became a vegetarian because of her disagreement with the way food is produced. I agree with her when she states that the way our food is farmed in the United States is affecting us adversely. But I drew the line when it came to giving up meat and fish. Fortunately, she was not insistent that the rest of the family also became vegetarians as I am sure that I would have become a closet carnivore! Sabrina researches and reads up on the subject, and ensures that our family eats the fruits, vegetables, and herbs that help us all to stay healthy. She is so committed to this that our 9- and 10-year-old kids have never been on antibiotics. I am thankful for my wife's commitment.

Amongst her many favorite books is *Life Changing Foods*.[1] It seems that any ailment I ever complain of can be alleviated by the different foods, herbs, and spices she suggests. However, a recurring remedy is cinnamon.

At first, this baffled me. I started to doubt all her suggestions. Cinnamon, a cure-all? There was no way. But I did my own research and found out that this is, indeed, an amazing spice. Cinnamon is a good remedy for a litany of things—from nausea, arthritis, lowering cholesterol, regulating

Dream Catcher, pages 17–21
Copyright © 2019 by Information Age Publishing
17

blood sugar to increasing blood circulation. I even learned that cinnamon has anti-carcinogenic properties and has been known to reduce the growth of leukemia and lymphoma cancer cells within the body.

Dream Catcher, however, is not cinnamon. It is not a cure-all for every ailment facing every organization.

I have spent a great deal of time learning and listening to executives who are part of groups such as Entrepreneurs Organization, Young Presidents' Organization, and Vistage (the world's leading executive coaching organization). They are part of those groups because they can talk with other executives who are able to share experiences and help each other through shared challenges. Most organizations have gone through struggles that others can learn from. Having heard how others have dealt with particular problems, they may well attempt to deploy the same tools or resources in their own organizations and expect the outcomes to be the same. For many, this approach will not be successful. Each organization is different and depending on its culture the way that problems should be addressed may vary.

Reading this book will certainly be helpful for such executives in some respects. When I consider an organization to work with I assess whether or not Dream Catcher is the right fit for them. Even when I see issues that I have successfully helped another organization with, I don't automatically believe that the same approach will work everywhere. To some, it seems like a bad decision to reject a client when an effortless copy and paste process could be utilized. However, I have come to understand, accept, and appreciate that Dream Catcher is not right for every organization.

Dream Catcher was designed to be effective in particular environments, atmospheres, and cultures. It is for organizations that operate with an unquestionable belief that their people are their biggest resource—businesses that have an unwavering commitment to investing in their teams.

Eighty percent of executives believe that their organization is in the top 10% of companies that are committed to their team members. But for many, this is just wishful thinking. Dream Catcher should be applied in organizations where such thinking is backed by real and demonstrable action.

Another factor that affects whether or not Dream Catcher will succeed is the leadership structure in an organization. Companies that operate with relatively few layers of management hierarchy are ideal. I look at the way a business is structured before deciding whether Dream Catcher can be helpful to them. If you look at the organizational chart, the taller the structure is, the further you get from compatibility with Dream Catcher's effectiveness. When there are too many layers from top to bottom, there is an automatic, and often institutionalized, deference to power that is difficult to overcome. Dream Catcher aims to empower individual team members. A flatter organizational structure always makes this more achievable. Even when a company with a hierarchical system works hard to try and keep its people empowered, it is a constant uphill battle.

Complex chains of command that focus on following directives are a mismatch for Dream Catcher. "Would you prefer a dictatorship or a true leadership team approach in running your business?" asks *Traction* author, Gino Wickman.[2] Both leadership systems can work but a dictatorship is exhausting and impedes the future growth of the organization. Dictatorships are dependent on simply telling others what to do. They obstruct opportunities for people to develop and for the company to position itself for succession planning. If you are a leader who would rather have their company operate like a dictatorship, stop reading now. Dream Catcher will be a waste of your time.

The smallest company that Dream Catcher has worked with has seven team members and the largest has 400. It is a very customizable program and can be modeled to suit the organization, as long as the organization suits it. When successfully applied, Dream Catcher leads to a culture of decentralized communication. The results I have seen include a move to truly open dialogue between leaders and the people in the organization. Relationships become richer as the communication is not within a chain, but rather happens cross-functionally. These organizations have developed rapid, reliable modes of communication that members gather straight from the source, regardless of their title and role. The program faces challenges when faced with rigid organizational structures where information comes through bulletins, memos, and company-wide emails.

If a company is not compatible with the program, the coaching methods can lead to developments that some organizations don't like. At QLI, for example, the people most affected by a decision are part of the decision-making process. This is a concept that some executives I have spoken with shy away from. They want to remain in control and yielding any sort of power to employees is scary for them. The coaching program can help leaders who are open to change and, usually through their own coaching process, learn how to take a more open and relaxed approach to team members. In essence, Dream Catcher can equip such leaders to yield control where necessary and help facilitate shared decision-making processes which are centered around and prioritize the company's mission. This is not possible when the dictatorial approach holds sway because of a leader's value system.

Because of these factors, I have made a commitment about the type of organizations I will work with. It is an unfair waste of time and resources for an organization to try and make the program work where it will likely fail.

This book's objectives do not include making a case against hierarchical structures in organizations. There are probably other coaching programs for those systems that will continue to exist in years to come and remain important for such companies to execute their own unique missions.

Born Free!

"History is written by the victors," proclaimed Winston Churchill. That was certainly the case when I was growing up and being taught the history of post-independence Zimbabwe.

Colonialism, just like slavery and apartheid, is a sensitive topic that has been skirted over and inaccurately documented with omission and euphemism. The colonization of a continent was justified by the European powers as being a necessity. To them, Europe was exporting civilization to countries that they regarded as being backward and undeveloped. My parents and three of my older siblings lived in British-controlled Rhodesia in an environment of oppression and propaganda that supported the status quo. After 13 years of insurrection, bloodshed, and war with its colonizers, Zimbabwe gained its independence.[3] April 18, 1980 ended almost a century of British-sponsored rule over the nation.[4]

I was born after Zimbabwe's independence and like everyone else who was born after that day, I was known as a "Born Free."

It was after independence that my family moved from the segregated high-density suburbs of the capital, Harare, to Bulawayo and the much more pleasant neighborhood of Montrose. My parents were able to purchase a home with a yard and even a swimming pool that also had a child-friendly pool for me, the youngest.

When we eventually returned to Harare, I attended Groombridge Primary (Elementary), a school that had been reserved for white kids when Zimbabwe was segregated just seven years earlier.[5]

Growing up with both of my parents working while also running a farm in rural Zimbabwe gave me an early glimpse into the world of work. We were certainly not wealthy when compared to the diplomats, doctors, and politicians that lived in our neighborhood. It was a wonderful place to grow up—great friends, safe streets to ride bikes on, and parents, who, in addition to consistently working hard to provide for the family, worked equally as hard to provide love in our home.

Like many Zimbabweans, we had domestic workers in our household, especially since both of my parents worked. One of the domestic workers was a maid for household chores. Her duties included cooking, cleaning, laundry (which was usually hand-washed and hung out to dry), ironing, folding, and putting away clothes. If you had young children in the family, as we did, the role also included being the child-minder. The domestic workers at our house were pretty much a part of our family. My parents demanded that my siblings and I respected and thanked them accordingly.

If you had a bigger yard like we did, it was also typical to have a gardener who tended to the yard with inefficient tools such as a slasher and sickle to cut the grass. He would maintain shrubbery, landscape, and generally tend to the garden. Many homes, including ours, also used their gardens to grow food for subsistence. As a young boy, I found it odd how it was my responsibility to tend to the garden on weekends and on school breaks. The "boss's child" laboring in the garden was an anomaly in Zimbabwe and because my parents made me work the garden I completely disagreed with the notion of myself as a "Born Free."

Looking back, I see these experiences helped shape the person I am today. I am proud of how my parents raised me. I am thankful for them prioritizing the need to make sure that we grew up with respect for our employees and in a home full of love.

Notes

1. William, A. (2016). Medical medium life-changing foods: Save yourself and the ones you love with the hidden healing powers of fruits and vegetables. Carlsbad, CA: Hay House.
2. Wickman, G. (2012) *Traction: Get a grip on your business.* Dallas, TX: Benbella Books.
3. http://www.worldhistory.biz/sundries/39661-zimbabwe-second-chimurenga-1966-1979.html
4. Bute, E. L., & Harmer, H. J. P. (1997). *The Black handbook.* London, England: Cassell; Fraser, R. (1998). *Keesing's records of world events: News digest for November 1995.* P. 42596 London, England: Longman.
5. Scenes in Rhodesia after desegregation in 1978. (2015, August 10). Retrieved from https://www.bbc.com/news/av/world-africa-33818664/scenes-in-rhodesia-after-desegregation-in-1978

3

Culture

The Most Important Part of Your Business

Culture: (noun)

The customs, arts, social institutions, and achievements of a particular nation, people, or other social group.

The attitudes and behavioral characteristics of a particular social group.[1]

The Culture I Found:

The concept of Dream Catcher is certainly the sum of all of the experiences I have had in my life. Over my two decades at QLI, together with my many colleagues, I have learned from all of the hardships and challenges that we have faced, and taken strength from the successes. I have been a part of a culture where people are the most valued resource. There is a true belief and commitment to people reaching their fullest potential. This program has been distilled from these many situations, lessons, and observations. I am a beneficiary of the people who invested in me. I may be a curious

Dream Catcher, pages 23–33
Copyright © 2019 by Information Age Publishing
23

and passionate person, but this has come from being encouraged to be so. Other people have helped inspire me to be the person I am today.

This same truth applies to Dream Catcher. It is effective in the right organizational culture. I have spoken to business leaders who were persuaded to adopt particular practices, processes, and programs because they had proved effective in other businesses. Organizations generally don't want to reinvent the wheel. After all, many of the best ideas are borrowed. But these same leaders also reported how such programs completely failed in their organizations.

The sports world has many examples of such failures. Teams often pay high prices for a player who was dominant for a rival only to discover that their new star signing isn't a good fit for the system. Big Ben Wallace's $60 million move to the Chicago Bulls, or the $100 million, including $41 million guaranteed, that the Washington Redskins paid for Albert Haynesworth turned out to be highly unproductive investments. No one foresaw these costly transactions ending in disappointment, even though success can never be guaranteed. However, if the buyers had scratched the surface a little deeper to really understand what these players needed to make them as successful as they had been for their previous teams, the outcome might have been different.

Dream Catcher is not a $100 million investment for your organization, but it is also important to investigate before you take the plunge. You should understand the environments in which it has been successful and why this has been the case. Before adopting the Dream Catcher program there are a number of steps you should take, which I will discuss in the next section.

Create the Right Culture

How to Build a Culture of Coaching

As you may already have acknowledged, your organization needs a culture of coaching for your employees for it to continue to thrive and achieve its purpose. Without this, Dream Catcher cannot succeed.

Building a coaching culture will help with the introduction of new systems so that change is received with an open mind and your team is ready and receptive to take on new ideas and make them successful. Some business owners assume that simply paying their employees' wages is enough for them to buy into new ideas that the leadership believes will make the company successful. But unless your employees feel valued as important elements in how the organization functions, change is more likely to create divisiveness between leaders and employees.

It is very possible to develop and improve any organizational culture. It is a challenging, yet manageable process. But first, you must understand that this is a process of change.

Be a Change Agent

Working at QLI, I learned many valuable lessons from the founder, Dr. Kim Hoogeveen, and often heard him say, "Change leads to conflict and conflict leads to change." What he was espousing was something that an-thropologists and organizational behavior experts have observed over the years. Change is a concept that is problematic for any organization that seeks to develop and not remain stagnant.

Since opening its doors in 1990, QLI embraced the idea of change by committing to continual excellence. Being open to change is something that QLI team members must have as an inherent quality if they are going to succeed. As a result, turnover at the company is very low—many people have been there for decades. QLI hires individuals who are assessed as be-ing open to change; but more importantly, QLI is renowned for how metic-ulously change is enacted. There are times when, as a leader, I have rushed through the process of making what I consider to be a simple change, by-passing the principles I was taught to apply. Without fail, this was not a smooth process.

If you fail to follow the following steps when enacting any change pro-cess, it is highly likely that the initiative will miss its mark.

1) Lead From the Front

If you want people to wholeheartedly buy into an idea, mandating how it will work in advance is not the way to go. Good leaders inspire others to follow them to the proverbial "promised land." If you lead by example, your employees will fol-low.[2] Dream Catcher is just like any other innovative idea that will succeed or fail de-

> "AS GOES THE LEADER, SO GOES THE ORGANIZATION."
>
> —John Maxwell

pending on whether an organization's leaders are advocates who can speak to the value it has for them personally.

2) Pull Them Under the Tent[3]

Organizations often make the mistake of announcing things via emails and bulletins. This is a sure way to guarantee that even the brightest and best ideas are likely to be unpopular and eventually rejected in any organization. Instead, what I have learned is that by encouraging people who will be directly affected by a new idea or change to be involved in the process at an early stage, the chances of success are greatly improved. This was a tactic often used at QLI by Dr. Hoogeveen, who may tell an employee: "I have something that isn't public knowledge that I'd like to share with you, because I value you." This creates immediate buy-in from the employee as they recognize the value that is being placed on them. It worked wonders on me despite later finding out that he had shared the same "news" with several others.

3) Start With Why[4]

Simon Sinek has a company that specializes in change management. The error that many organizations make, according to Sinek, is that by just explaining *what* is happening and *how* it will be implemented, ignores the *why*. When endeavoring to get buy-in from employees for a change process, it is imperative that you focus and lead with the "why." You must sell that first and foremost to get big picture understanding.

In the case of Dream Catcher, imagine that this is the "why":

"We have the opportunity to more effectively execute our company's mission and invest in all of our team members."

Next, transition to the "what" and "how."

"We will be a part of a simple-to-use program that will help us further invest in our team members. The program will equip us with methods to help individually define where we ideally want to be professionally and personally. It will also help us navigate that path with confidence."

Starting with "why" does two things—it makes "what" and "how" easier to identify. And it keeps your end goal in your sights.

4) Ask, Consider, Address

When I was "pulled under the tent," I felt that my opinion was valuable. It created an environment where I felt able to openly share my point of view and feelings on a number of issues. I was asked what I thought and how I felt about whatever impending change was coming. I happily shared my unfiltered thoughts and asked questions. After all, I felt like I was speaking to someone who had shown me that they cared.

When I had concerns, I aired them and they were carefully considered. Given that I am in a role to help enact change and have a better understanding of the process than many others, my concerns were mostly taken seriously and not quickly rebutted. I was assured that they would be given more consideration. Fully including employees in the change process is good strategy for any organization.

As the process evolved I was told how my concerns had been handled. Even if the feedback didn't support my concerns, I felt that they had been properly addressed. The company cared enough not only to listen, but also take the time to consider my suggestions and get back to me. I was important enough and worthy of the time. That seemed to me to override whatever concerns I had with the bigger picture—the change that was coming. I became an advocate for the change. I bought into and trusted what was going to happen. I championed it along with others who had also been pulled under the tent.

5) Decision Day

It may appear that the time is right to usher in whatever change is needed. Instead, caution must be taken. There are, at times, people who, despite having been pulled under the tent, remain dissenters. They may be key opinion leaders who can impact how effective the change process will be. Alternatively, they may be quiet-yet-valuable team members who may become disengaged. This is the perfect time to spend more time with them. Listen a little more and commit to understanding where they are coming from. It may be the case that they have valid points that should take precedence over the suggested change. If not, it is time for further analysis.

If the dissenters are still compromising the change process or could sabotage the outcomes once the change is effected, ask whether or not these individuals are more important than the organization and its objectives. The likely answer is, of course, no. Just like companies who prioritize their mission, it will be time for these individuals to make a decision. They will either move on in full support of the change or they will need to find another organization to work for that suits the status quo they wish to retain.

Change is handled so exceptionally at QLI that such outcomes are extremely rare. But for any organization, the unapologetic upholding of its mission must come first.

> **NOTE!**
>
> This method of ushering in change is not a fast process. It has no shortcuts. But when compared to mandating change, the outcomes and their by-products are more than worthwhile. Organizations that care about the voices of their employees and value their engagement will benefit from the increased pride and loyalty shown by their teams. This is how QLI has become and will continue to be an organization that many people want to work for.

How to Develop a Culture of Transparency

If the steps needed to create a culture of coaching are followed with discipline, the results will lead to a higher level of trust within the organization. Trust is not a commodity one can buy; it must be earned. It is the role of the leaders in the organization to earn the trust of their team members. Lies and secrets break trust. Dream Catcher is a program that has been effective in organizations with high levels of trust. I highly recommend coaches read Stephen Covey's book *The Speed of Trust* as a resource on how to quickly build, maintain, and, if it's compromised, rebuild trust.[5]

With trust comes transparency. To effectively coach someone, they must realize that there are gaps that exist between where they currently are and where they want to be. The Dream Catcher program uses techniques that lead to such self-discovery. The program also continually evaluates the client's progress. This means being honest and direct. Many aspects of Dream Catcher, including identifying the gaps, introducing accountability, and evaluating progress involve transparency. For this to work within an organization, it is essential that there is a transparent and open culture. The attitudes and behavior of the leadership must be consistent.

Business leaders have known about the benefits of a culture of trust and openness for many years and some have taken the idea further and built great organizational cultures. But for others, the challenge has been how, exactly, to do it.

Culture: From Day 1

A small group of exceptional companies like QLI have invested in creative and engaging methods that continue to keep the culture rich and consistent. The QLI team loves it when other organizations come to visit and hear about the philosophy that has helped build its success. When the methods are shared there is an opportunity to elevate standards in other organizations. One concept that has helped the QLI culture become instilled in all team members and fostered over time is the way that the process begins on Day 1.

On the first day of work, every new team member is paired up with a seasoned and committed team member known as a Q-Link. It is the Q-Link's role to get to know the new team member and help them become familiar and comfortable with the company as they establish themselves. The Q-Link pairing is formally set up for 6 weeks, however, it has organically evolved into very close relationships that have stood the test of time and transcended into life in general. This system—created by Jill Vollmuth, QLI's director of skill building, and her small team—has led not only to new team members quickly feeling connected to the mission of the organization and understanding how to grow personally within QLI, but also to veteran team members reporting that they find even more purpose in their already enriching work.

There is also a range of mentoring programs geared to help employees from varying backgrounds, levels of experience, and job roles through diverse learning styles. Team members learn and understand the QLI culture, begin to feel empowered, and are guided towards resources to achieve what they strive for. It is no surprise that, just like myself, every single leader at this company has progressed from entry-level roles and fosters the same open spirit for newcomers. QLI continues to be an innovative mission-focused talent incubator.

▬▬▬▬

Their Vision is Your Mission

The mission of QLI is to deliver life-changing rehabilitation and care: to protect dignity, instill purpose, and create hope with a commitment to excellence.

In 2017, I read an article in *Forbes* that started me on a personal quest. The article asserted that corporate mission statements are useless without a great leader.[6] Most organizations have mission statements, and I began asking business leaders from a range of industries about what theirs meant to them. These were all well-known and very profitable companies, some of which are nationally and internationally known. There was a consistent theme in the responses. Most people in senior leadership roles knew what their company mission was, but they also felt that the actions within their organizations often didn't match this defining statement of why they existed.

If the mission statement bears no resemblance to what actually happens within an organization, is it of any value?

As a national provider of rehabilitation services, QLI is subject to rigorous systems that assess and ensure it meets certain criteria via accreditation. One of those systems is The Commission on Accreditation of Rehabilitation Facilities (CARF).[7] CARF is an independent, international nonprofit organization focused on advancing the quality of services in order to achieve successful outcomes for people in rehabilitation facilities. The providers that become CARF-accredited need to demonstrate that they are among the best rehabilitation providers. QLI has been a perennial preferred rehabilitation provider in the United States.

In 2018, QLI hosted CARF assessors in order to complete the comprehensive renewal process. The team analyzed the entire rehab program, our organizational systems, including but certainly not limited to hiring practices, onboarding, training, and general organizational effectiveness.

The assessors were collaborative and helpful and spent time sifting through the documentation QLI provided as well as interviewing team members, the clients we serve, along with members of their families. They also took time to personally observe our organizational practices by attending meetings. They left no stone unturned. This very thorough process ended with the assessors commenting that they were amazed at our rehabilitation program and they had no recommendations on how to improve it. One key thing that they observed in their time at QLI was how every team member that they interacted with knew the mission statement. From newer entry-level staff to long-time team members, the mission was something that was reiterated over and over to them. They were struck by how the mission shaped every action within the program. A mission can be an organization's greatest asset if it is genuine and truly lived by its people.

Over the time I have been employed at QLI, I have had many great experiences because of that unified approach to the mission. I am fortunate to work every day with individuals who care about our values and, in turn, genuinely care about each other. I would invite anyone who would like to take a tour to come and visit anytime to experience how a mission-led organization works. In a desert of terrible, toxic work cultures, QLI is an oasis.

Having said that, QLI is by no means perfect. However, because there is a constant drive towards excellence, it continues to be a place where shortcomings aren't ignored. I have had my own growing pains over the last 18 years and I do not anticipate that the future will be any different regarding the challenges and opportunities that adversity will provide.

The Problem With Millennials

I have talked with several leaders who work with the younger group of employees joining their workforce. Their complaints about millennials have waned with time but still persist. Some of the issues with millennials that have been raised include their lack of values, their emphasis on work–life balance, that they want everything for nothing, that they are entitled, and that they lack loyalty.

At QLI, over 50% of the employees are millennials and we have solved these so-called problems. How? By being a people-centric organization. When you focus on people, they will in turn focus on you. The theory of reciprocity, studied by behavioral scientists for years, applies to every aspect of your business.[8] Dream Catcher is very focused on reciprocity. Coaching should be done with a focus on the vision and needs of your client. When you have invested in them to discover their vision, the gaps they wish to close, and the areas they want to become experts in, the process is all about them and how they can help your business excel.

Motivation: What Many Don't Understand

Hoosiers, Rocky, Friday Night Lights, Any Given Sunday. These movies have a number of things in common. One obvious factor is that they are all iconic sports films, but they also have similarities in terms of their themes and how they play out. All have an underdog who, for cinematic purposes, is set to wildly outperform expectations. The road to success is, of course, not straightforward. In all of these films the underdog has to have been firstly utterly dominated by an adversary with victory seemingly impossible.

In this bleak filmic moment, all hope appears to be lost. But wait! Here is *the speech*. The coach talks to the individual or team and fires them up with passion. Suddenly, there is an epic comeback and a fight for the ages. The Hollywood trope of improbable success suggests that the coach has motivated his player or players to fight and give it their all. Given how pervasive these stories are it is not strange that business leaders call for action in a similar fashion, searching for the perfect speech to motivate their workforce and improve results. But Hollywood is an inaccurate and romantic portrayal of how motivation works. Sadly, in life, and unfortunately, also in business, people misunderstand what motivation actually is.

Motivation is an intrinsic force. It is far from the fervor-filled halftime speech or the desire to attain a short-term goal or target. A vision without action is nothing more than a daydream.

From an organizational behavior perspective, motivation consists of three major components: activation, persistence, and intensity.[9]

1. *Activation* involves the decision to **initiate** a behavior.
2. *Persistence* is the continued **effort** toward a goal in spite of obstacles.
3. *Intensity* is reflected by unwavering **focus** and **drive**.

For anyone to ever succeed they must be determined and they must persevere. In short, they must be motivated! As Warren Buffet has said, "Intensity is the price of excellence."

In his book, Simon Sinek stresses how it is not the leader's role to motivate people.[10] Instead, he argues that leaders should hire people who are already motivated and inspire them. As a Dream Catcher coach, you are the leader. To coach someone effectively, the client must already be motivated—not in the Hollywood sense of the word or what people look for from "motivational speakers." Instead, your comprehension of the three components of motivation will help you select the right candidates for coaching who will, in turn, shape and influence the potency of your coaching. You cannot and should never attempt to coach an unmotivated person.

People wonder how the organizations that use Dream Catcher are able to attract, recruit, and retain exceptional talent.

It's simple!

Motivated people are attracted to organizations that will, at the very least, realize and appreciate their potential as individuals. More importantly, they want to work for organizations that will help inspire and elevate them through coaching. A company that is known as a great place to work because of a reputation for inspiring its motivated team members will soon be highly sought after by other equally motivated people. Dream Catcher can provide your company with a never-ending conveyor belt of motivated talent that will not want to leave.

The best executives take time to consider and think about the future of their organization. They want to ensure that their company can thrive beyond their time as a leader through effective succession planning. If highly motivated talent is attracted to the company it is automatically positioned advantageously for such issues. There will already be a deep talent pool to coach the next wave of leaders to take the company to new heights.

Notes

1. Webster, N. (1963). "Culture" in *New Collegiate Dictionary: Merriam-Webster*. Springfield, MA: G. & C. Merriam.
2. Schindler, J. (2015). *Followership: What it takes to lead*. New York, NY: Business Expert Press.
3. MindSet: A Tour Through the Mind of Exceptional Leaders. (n.d.). Retrieved from http://gomindset.com/
4. Home. (n.d.). Retrieved August 25, 2018, from https://startwithwhy.com/
5. Covey, S. M. (2006). *The speed of trust*. New York, NY: Free Press.
6. Sherman, L. (2017, April 3). *Corporate mission statements don't really matter, unless you want to be a great leader*. Retrieved from https://www.forbes.com/sites/lensherman/2017/04/03/corporate-mission-statements-dont-really-matter-unless-you-want-to-be-a-great-leader/#59af18ef2246
7. http://www.carf.org/home/
8. Avolio, B. J., & Yammarino F. J. (2013). Introduction to, and overview of, transformational and charismatic leadership. In *Transformational and charismatic leadership: The road ahead* (10th anniversary ed.). Bingley, UK: Emerald.
9. Nevid, J. (2013). *Psychology: Concepts and applications*. Belmont, CA: Wadworth.
10. Sinek, S. (2013). *Start with why: How great leaders inspire everyone to take action*. London, England: Portfolio/Penguin.

4

The Worldview of a Winning Coach

How do you see the world? Your approach to leadership is very likely an indicator of how you view human behavior. Your leadership style directly correlates to your attitudes, assumptions, and core beliefs about what makes those you lead, tick. The same applies to the way you coach. After all, coaching is an element of leadership.

Assess the way in which you view the people who report to you directly. You will find that the way you view them is less a result of their actions, but rather the perceived value you place in them.

> "THE MEDIOCRE TEACHER TELLS. THE GOOD TEACHER EXPLAINS.
>
> THE SUPERIOR TEACHER DEMONSTRATES.
>
> THE GREAT TEACHER INSPIRES."
>
> —William Arthur Ward

As a by-product of my time at QLI, I have learned from outstanding individuals such as Dr. Kim Hoogeveen, the founder and now-former CEO of the company. Dr. Hoogeveen is now working with his new venture, Mindset LLC.[1] During his tenure at QLI, he shared several books with us. As a result, one of my favorite business minds in history has become Arie de Geus, who

Dream Catcher, pages 35–44

35

popularized the notion of the "Living Company" in his landmark book of the same name.[2] In it, de Geus suggests that in mechanistic systems, managers concern themselves with land, labor, and capital while neglecting the important fact that labor equates to real people. This mechanistic focus, according to de Geus, has caused many companies to fail. To discover how companies could flourish, de Geus analyzed a 1983 study, undertaken by oil and gas company Shell, that inspected time-tested companies to learn lessons about long-term corporate survival. The goal was to replicate their methods to help Shell—already more than a century old—continue to thrive. What the study found was that globally, the few companies that had existed for over a century did not view their employees as mere cogs in the system. They valued them as key elements in ensuring their success.

There are many organizations where mechanistic systems hold sway. If yours is such a company, placing no value on your people other than as human work communities, you as a leader are a dinosaur—and your organizations' days are likely to be numbered.

Dream Catcher's methods guide organizations towards becoming living companies—not mechanistic ones. Dream Catcher refers to leaders who use methods that cause organizations to die off as "Primitive Leaders." Instead, it is important to strive to be the type of leader that Dream Catcher refers to as "Transformative"—leaders who embrace those they hire as more than just "labor"; as real people who are essential in contributing to and fulfilling the mission of the organization.

Primitive Leaders

When people are merely seen as cogs in the company machinery, your organization is unhealthy. If your belief is that your company, team, or group is populated with individuals who inherently dislike applying themselves, struggle with effort, lack ambition, and need to be constantly supervised, your leadership style will reflect that. You will likely be rigid, dictatorial, and directive. Your role as a leader will be to actively intervene to get things done. You will run a system where people need your authority to operate. This is primitive leadership.

Transformative Leaders

If you believe that the people you lead are driven, want to learn and grow, and have a deep desire to be a part of something bigger than themselves you will be in the position to nurture an exhilarating organization. Arie de Geus analogizes such organizations to a living organism. You will find that as a leader, you have a voracious and insatiable appetite to create a transformative and participative system. One that people truly feel invested in as members and partners—an organization designed to develop *with* them.

The biggest obstacles that a coach faces when following the Dream Catcher process are created because they are likely looking at their clients through a primitive leadership lens. The coaching process will not work if the organization's culture is based on following rigid systems in order for an individual to operate. Often, you are coaching a person who is supervised by someone else. Even in systems that are transformative, a particular manager may have a more primitive outlook. Try and address such issues when you find them. The success of both your client and the company that they work for depends on their adeptness to effectively lead—and being allowed the space to do that.

Choosing the Right Client

A few years ago, when Dream Catcher was still in its infancy, I coached a few leaders at QLI. These were people that I had hand-selected to test elements of the program. Chris was a director that I had previously worked with and was extremely valuable as a beta tester. She later became one of the first trained Dream Catcher coaches. Chris supervised a young woman, Kristin, who had just started at the company in an entry-level role as a rehab trainer.

Even though the coaching program wasn't yet formalized, Chris was familiar with the philosophy behind it and the required traits of the ideal coaching candidate. She asked that I connect with Kristin just to get acquainted.

When I first met Kristin, I found her to be a very socially skilled, bright, and witty person. She was engaging and shared a few personal details that I found impressive. I shared a little of my life—my move to the United States, and my career path at QLI.

Kristin had a healthy sense of ambition along with a deep passion for the mission of QLI and the work she did in transforming lives that had been negatively impacted after a catastrophic injury. She worked full time and also attended Creighton University where she was completing a master's in public health with the goal of becoming an epidemiologist.

We talked about how the public health field has been slow to progress beyond major crises—industry epidemics including opioid abuse, obesity, and the challenges surrounding HIV/AIDS. Although we agreed, Kristin remained optimistic, encouraging me to believe in a future where people like her would make a difference.

She shared news about her fiancé, who she is now married to. How they had grown up together in Georgia and now planned to make Omaha their home. I am notorious for asking people many questions as I get to know them, but Kristin was comfortable in sharing and very open, so I continued.

As I started to understand her ambitions and what success meant for her in her life, I asked her something that every coach must ask a potential client. What were some of the hurdles she would have to overcome to succeed? This seldom happens in a first meeting, as it is something you want your client to reflect on. If you ask too early you tend to get a shallow answer. That's what I expected from Kristin, but I was wrong!

I saw a different side to her. She burst into tears. She shared how her previous experiences had affected her and were hurdles that she still had to overcome. Her personal beliefs and internal dialogue were tremendous obstacles. She didn't say it directly, but it was clear that her confidence was low. It severely affected how she viewed the world and in turn dealt with conflict, both at work and in her life. In subsequent meetings we would discuss this in great detail.

The meeting had been planned to get to know each other a little, but she had been brave and her authentic self. Even through the tears, she pushed on to say that she wanted help in overcoming this internal dialogue—a voice that compromised her belief in her true abilities.

Not just because she was open, vulnerable, and emotional from the first meeting, Kristin remains one of my favorite people I have coached. She helped lay the foundations for some important principles that make Dream Catcher the potent program it is today.

Every session that we met was rich in terms of what was discussed and how we agreed to proceed. Kristin's personal drive and zeal taught me what the roles of both a coach and client must be; to be successful, both parties need to commit and be willing to work very hard.

The tears affirmed that the client has to know, before starting, that the process is going to be emotionally tough. When Kristin would do things that were far outside her comfort zone, I learned that it was exactly at that moment that she was growing the most.

For every hour I spent with Kristin, despite the fact that she had a full-time job and was pursuing her master's, she would commit to at least 10 hours of work at home. At first I was shocked but soon realized that a coach must never be as underprepared as I initially was. It also revealed to me that the coach/client relationship should yield a high return on the coach's time investment. Kristin's drive inspired me to challenge myself more. A Dream Catcher coach who is committed to inspiring the full potential of others must also be prepared to severely stretch their own capabilities.

As I continued to work with Kristin, Chris also became involved. We collaborated and had great intellectual dialogs about Kristin, her path, and the process. We worked together, making sure that what we were both doing was aligned and would translate into practice. In addition to Kristin's work on self-reflection, Chris was an extra set of eyes helping her in the day-to-day workplace. That also helped me understand how Kristin was doing outside of our coaching sessions.

Kristin spent time with other people in the company, establishing relationships with several individuals she didn't typically work with. These included Patricia Kearns, the president and CEO of QLI. Spending time with team members is something Patricia loves and commits to doing. This, of course, is also extremely helpful. For Dream Catcher to be successful, it is imperative that the program is endorsed and vigorously supported at the highest levels of the company.

Kristin subsequently grew as a person and ascended QLI's unique career ladder in her role as a rehab trainer. After completing her master's in public health she had many opportunities to go and work in the field that she had studied but decided to stay at QLI. At the time of writing this book, she is QLI's compliance specialist, responsible for ensuring QLI's clinical services meet the demanded state and federal regulations expected of care facilities in our industry.

It would be easy to correlate the different roles that Kristin has gone on to hold directly to working with me as a coach. This, however, is not the case. All of the new roles that Kristin took on were earned after our coaching relationship ended. A good coach is one who instills good principles and methods so that their clients can effectively close The Gap between where they are and where they want to be. Success as a Dream Catcher coach means helping clients to succeed independently. Clients must take the principles from the program and apply them to their lives.

If you expect most coaching interactions to go as smoothly as my experience with Kristin, you are being unrealistic. It can be a challenge to decide on who the right person is when it comes to selecting the right candidate to coach.

In order to make this challenging process clearer, I have created a checklist to help coaches create a profile of the ideal potential client.

The traits I believe are important are associated with the motivated individuals Dream Catcher has consistently had success with. It is vital that your organization makes it a priority to hire individuals who are coachable and open to learning. This can still prove to be a challenge, even for those with rigorous and very competitive interviewing and selection processes.

Good companies have done a reasonable job in identifying their top performers and developing them. Where there is a problem is in helping those that are neither the best or worst performers. This "middle group" of humble and not as visible team members tends to be the most populated group. Managers I have spoken with have cited many reasons why they have failed to engage and enthuse this "middle group," including being too busy working with the squeaky wheels, having too much on their plate generally, and simply not knowing how to help. When asked if they knew how they would select whom to invest more development time in, they were unclear.

The Dream Catcher checklist provides coaches with a tool that they can apply to select the right client. Supervisors and managers baffled by where to start with their "middle group" have also benefited from using this tool.

For every trait listed below, there is also a point of caution. An accurate diagnosis and assessment of a potential client is important and this can sometimes be problematic. I have sometimes misread the signals. Looking back at some of those situations, I realize that I completely missed the signs that would have given me a more accurate picture. When doctors misdiagnose they do harm. The same applies to misdiagnosing during the client selection process. The coach should study the following essential traits when choosing a client, but also pay attention to the words of caution. If not, you could end up in a toxic and unproductive coaching partnership.

Traits of the Ideal Client

1) Passion

By definition, passion is an intense desire or enthusiasm for something. A passionate person has a deep desire to be successful at everything they do. In order for Dream Catcher to succeed, you must coach individuals who are intensely committed to the process, but don't make the error of dismissing individuals with a calm demeanor and a quieter spirit. Passion is not always exhibited loudly and with expressive zeal. Some people who are, perhaps, just a little more stoic, a little more introverted, and reserved are often seen as being dispassionate. This might be a complete misdiagnosis. A quieter person may also be someone who won't settle for second best and pursues excellence.

🔊 **Be cautious:** When you believe that you have identified a passionate individual, look closer. Make sure that the passion you are seeing is about their drive to develop and achieve success. Sometimes you will run into the type of person that I have labeled "the advocate." Such people will likely aggressively pursue their own personal agenda and interests. At organizations with a strong mission, such as QLI, the focus of all individuals is to be aligned with the organizational goals. That means a focus on serving the interest of clients, their families, funding sources, the community, and other team members, all simultaneously. Advocates tend to forget the overall mission and only pursue particular elements of their personal interests with passion. When they have finished fighting for a particular position or issue, the rest of the team has to get together and rectify whatever other ramifications their actions may have caused. Advocates are coachable, but they should be treated with caution.

2) Accomplishments

Look for people that have accomplished many things in their lives. This indicates that they are driven. Whether their achievements are academic, vocational, or through community involvement, such people get things done. They are high achievers!

🔊 **Be cautious:** I have always warned coaches and other leaders to be careful when assessing people based only on their accomplishments. In many organizations, people correlate accomplishment simply with academic achievements or credentials. There are some people who have had academic success that you should be wary about in terms of whether they are suitable for coaching. The problem is that some academic high-achievers place more value on themselves than the organization or its mission.

3) Resilience/Agility

Resilience when combined with a level of agility is a potent combination. Always seek out the person who is both tough and agile. These individuals are very coachable as they process new ideas quickly and tend to see the opportunities in adversity.

🔊 **Caution:** If you identify these traits in an individual, be on the lookout for the hero syndrome or the all-too-dangerous self-promoting martyr. These people tend to create problems just to show how valuable they are in resolving them.

4) Optimism

Dream Catcher coaching is effective when working with individuals whose mental attitude reflects a belief in and hope for a favorable outcome. These individuals also tend to exhibit agility and resilience when things are not as rosy as they could be. They are able to look at a challenge and see it as a potential opportunity. Find such individuals and you will have clients who really believe that they can succeed. Your ideal client should be optimistic *and* spirited, able to bounce back from adversity, and focused on the positives. Such people don't let the fear of repeating their mistakes paralyze them, or worse, lead them into depressive moods.

📢 **Caution:** There is a difference between optimism and seeing the world through rose-tinted spectacles. Some apparent optimists are unrealistic and fail to recognize real dangers or legitimate concerns. They believe that "everything is awesome." There are also those that are merely faking or feigning optimism. This is a really, really difficult trait to spot and to validate.

5) Openness

Humans generally like to have clarity, but sometimes, there simply aren't any answers to the questions we have. They simply do not exist. Yet, because of this desire for definition, some people choose to live within the black and white parameters of life. Such people can at times find coaching difficult as the process involves plenty of thinking outside of the box and venturing outside of the comfort zone. As a coach, you want people who are, or can be, open to uncertainty. A client with an open mind is likely to be more receptive to trying new approaches and being comfortable with innovative learning.

📢 **Caution:** Some people who reject certainty are rebels who prefer to embrace chaos. They are so independent that they don't feel that any rules apply to them. Such individuals will, of course, be uncoachable.

6) Curiosity

A good client is someone who shows the zeal to learn something new every day. They are always asking "Why?" or "Tell me more" and are naturally inquisitive.

📢 **Caution:** You must be cautious of an insubordinate person that constantly asks "Why?" Their apparent curiosity is borne from a demand to "Justify this to me," or "Why should I do this?" When asked for a motive for their constant questioning, they will say that they are merely being inquisitive.

7) Persistence

Coaching is a difficult process, as at some point there will be a test of willpower between the coach and the client. This may be challenging and uncomfortable for the people that you coach. The process will not always be smooth and things will not always go perfectly. As the Zen proverb states, "Ride your horse along the edge of a sword; hide yourself in the middle of the flames." This process is not for the quitters. You want to coach the never-say-die type of individual.

🔊 **Caution:** When selecting a client and vetting them for the quality of persistence, be cautious of the lone wolf. These egocentric and self-absorbed "driven" people can lead a team off the edge of a cliff because they don't know when to pause. They don't investigate alternative paths even when the path decided on has developed treacherous hazards.

If you believe that a potential client is missing one or two of the traits and this makes them less than an ideal candidate, I suggest you do one of two things. Firstly, you could pair them with a mentor to work on those weaker traits so that they are more prepared for coaching. Secondly, you could bring them into the program and focus your work on the missing key traits so that they develop while in the program.

NOTE

When going through this process, I suggest that you ask a different person (or two) who is knowledgeable about the candidate to also consider the key traits and then compare notes with them.

To Coach or Not to Coach?

I started to formalize the Dream Catcher coaching system during its early stages in 2016. I had earlier been testing the application of the program with a few hand-selected people at QLI. A colleague of mine, Kinyarie, who I had worked with for many years, heard about the program.

She had previously been one of my mentors and had helped me grow as a person immensely.

She saw potential in a young man that she supervised and asked if I could help coach him. Hearing her speak so positively about him reminded me of why I had succeeded at the company—through the support of leaders who believe in people who may not yet believe in themselves.

I met with the potential client and after an in-depth discussion I politely told Kinyarie that I would have to decline to coach him. It left her confused. Why would we, as leaders who are committed to the success of others, not coach someone with potential? It appeared to be counterintuitive to how things are supposed to work at QLI.

I had been a direct benefactor of the patience and accommodation shown by QLI as they assisted me with my own shortcomings. I was an employee that had needed many chances due to my immaturity and lack of full commitment to the mission. Kinyarie had been one of the people who had invested their time and energy in me and had been directly instrumental to my success.

Dream Catcher was not for him. After Kinyarie and I discussed the way the program worked, she agreed with me. Instead, he went on to get some support through the mentoring program.

TABLE 4.1 The Differences Between Coaching and Mentoring			
Modality	**"What"** it looks like	**"How"** to do it	**"Why"** it's important
Mentoring	• Relationship oriented • Long-term • Development focus • Taking mentee under the wing	• Trust • Provide answers • Give solutions • Teach	• Organizational history • Experiential learning • Guidance • Use mentor as a resource
Coaching	• Task/goal oriented • Specified time or short-term • Performance focus • High ROI on coach's time	• Trust • Inspire • Radical candor • Clarity • Guidance	• Gap closure • Skill building • Growth • Learn to generalize

5

Do I Need to Make Them Happy?

A Coaching Pitfall

May the 4th Be With You!

May 4, 2016, is a day that I will not forget anytime soon.

I was sitting in a quiet restaurant called the Liberty Tavern, located in the Hilton Hotel in downtown Omaha, Nebraska. That morning, I happened to be reading a book and having breakfast. It was also a good spot to spend some time just before going across the street to the CenturyLink Center for the 8th grade honor roll ceremony sponsored by my rotary club.

Anthony, the waiter assigned to the section I decided to sit in, was someone I got the standard food service experience from. He took my order, brought the food out, and walked by twice asking if everything was ok. I had no complaints.

At 8:55 a.m. a middle-aged, fast-moving waitress named Jean zipped by my table and asked me a question that made this particular morning remarkable. "Are you happy?" she asked. What should have been a quick response—a mindless "Yes"—refused to come out and I took a bit more

Dream Catcher, pages 45–49
Copyright © 2019 by Information Age Publishing
All rights of reproduction in any form reserved.

time before I responded. Of course, I knew she was talking about the food. However, on this particular day, that particular question seemed fundamental to many other areas of my life. Was I happy?

I finally responded, "I am happy!" and went on to ask, "Are you happy?" Jean seemed caught off guard. The question left her with a slightly wry smile, and her eyebrows were raised high enough to accentuate the wrinkles on her forehead. I thought that my question had made her uncomfortable with the way it changed the tone of what would normally have been a humdrum discourse. But Jean looked pensive and was clearly thinking deeply. She took a pause, slightly tipped her head to the side, smiled, and made eye contact with me with the look of someone about to speak from the heart. With a faint squint of her eyes, and from what appeared to be deep within her soul, Jean said, "You know what? I am happy. Thanks for asking." I smiled back at her and watched her walk away at the speed she had been flying around at earlier.

I began to reflect on the notion of happiness. I contemplated why I was happy. Why was Jean happy? I didn't waste too much more time musing. Instead, I decided to invert the question: Why are so many people not? I started to ponder life's stressors, dissonances, and discord—the things that bring unhappiness.

What prevents people from finding "Happiness?"

Three Thoughts

1) Happiness is an Option

I have had the blessing at QLI of helping to rehabilitate the lives of individuals affected by severe brain or spinal cord injuries—people who may have never rediscovered hope after being robbed of the ability to walk, speak, live independently, or do the things they were once passionate about doing.

It is to be expected that they and their loved ones struggle to cope, let alone find happiness. Many would expect a work environment like QLI to be sad and sterile.

It is not!

Instead, QLI is an uplifting and harmonious place. The environment is a catalyst for so many positive things. I believe that occurs because so many people there choose the path of happiness. Along with the extensive cutting-edge rehabilitation services provided, the company helps clients and family members understand that, despite the physical limitations and challenges they may face, they are still in control of their lives. Nobody is in charge of your happiness except you!

I see men and women at QLI overcome their injuries, relearning how to walk, to speak, and to live independently. It is powerful to witness people accept some very difficult and challenging changes in their lives and adapt to their new circumstances. It is even more inspiring to see people overcome these challenges and return to their families, their jobs, and reclaim their passionate selves. I see so many of those individuals take charge of how they feel in such a stressful situation. They own it.

> "HAPPINESS IS A CHOICE, NOT A RESULT. NOTHING WILL MAKE YOU HAPPY UNTIL YOU CHOOSE TO BE HAPPY. NO PERSON WILL MAKE YOU HAPPY. YOUR HAPPINESS WILL NOT COME TO YOU. IT CAN ONLY COME FROM YOU."
>
> —Ralph Marston

The decision to seek and find happiness results in the amazing stories those of us at QLI witness.

2) Happiness is a Contagion

My personal guide and inspiration on many matters related to leadership is, as I've mentioned earlier in the book, Dr. Kim Hoogeveen. Preferring to go simply by the name "Kim" (rather than Dr. Hoogeveen), he founded QLI and led as President and CEO for two decades until 2010. The culture of the company is built on his leadership principles, which have also been a huge influence on my own understanding of the notion of leadership.

> "SOME CAUSE HAPPINESS WHEREVER THEY GO, OTHERS WHENEVER THEY GO."
>
> —Oscar Wilde

Dr. Hoogeveen's background in psychology, married with his passion for leadership culture, led to the creation of his new organization, MindSet LLC.[1] One of his most important MindSet concepts—"Stars versus Vacuums"—is very relevant when discussing happiness.

According to Hoogeveen, "Stars shine!" When they are around, they elevate the atmosphere, infuse energy, and bring life to any situation. At the other end of the spectrum there are the "Vacuums." They suck the life and energy from every situation or interaction in every room that they enter. Vacuums are unhappy and can proliferate the cancer of misery in an organization.

It is worth reflecting on the degree to which you impact others as a Star or a Vacuum: Are people happy *wherever* you go; or *whenever* you go?

3) "Happiness is an Inside Job"
—William Arthur Ward

Happiness is primarily about internal factors and depends only minimally on external matters. One of my favorite authors, George Orwell suggested that happiness can only exist with the acceptance of oneself.[2] Perhaps, with that in mind, if people see their lives in angst-ridden terms, if they are unsettled and unsatisfied, yet are doing nothing (or even worse, the wrong things) about it, misery will be their friend.

Lessons from May 4

Pat Hazell, a comedy writer who had worked on *Seinfeld,* was the keynote speaker for the 8th grade honor roll luncheon.[3] One thing that he shared at the end of his speech cemented the fact that happiness was the theme of the day. Hazell said, "Bad news, there is no key to happiness." He paused a while as people took that in before continuing. "Great news, the door isn't locked."

I agree with that diagnosis, but would elaborate a little more: there is no key to happiness because there is no door in the first place. It is a path. And the good news is that, for the many who haven't yet discovered how to be happy, there is a way to find that path and travel down it.

Happiness and Dream Catcher

As a Dream Catcher coach, it is important to understand happiness. Most coaches care very much about the people they work with and, at some point, this may result in them becoming involved when a client hits a rough patch in life. These coaches work hard to try and make their client happy with life. The discontentment of the client has in turn adversely affected the coach's attitude.

It is not the responsibility of a coach to make a client happy with his or her life. Don't fall into the trap of working for a client and suddenly finding yourself responsible for a person's happiness. Your role is to help your client discover their purpose and assist them in making the journey to discover their own opportunities to find happiness.

SUMMARY

Dream Catcher Organizational Prerequisites:

- Unquestionable and unwavering commitment to team members
- Non-dictatorial leaders
- Team member voices are heard and listened to
- Leaner and less hierarchical structure
- Culture of learning and coaching
- Culture of transparency

Coaches know:

- Dream Catcher is about inspiration, not motivation. Understanding the concept of motivation—initiation, effort, focus, and drive—is vital.
- Transformative leaders are capable of effective coaching.
- There is a particular set of personal traits one should look for in an ideal client.
- For those who don't have the right traits for coaching, try mentoring.
- There are key differences between mentoring and coaching.
- Dream Catcher coaches are not responsible for their client's "happiness."

Notes

1. MindSet | A Tour Through the Mind of Exceptional Leaders. (n.d.). Retrieved August 25, 2018, from http://gomindset.com/
2. Woodcock, G. (2018, June 21). George Orwell. Retrieved from https://www.britannica.com/biography/George-Orwell
3. From Here to Seinfeld: The Amazing Career of Pat Hazell (The Wonder Bread Years Runs December 19–22 at the Long Center). (2015, July 28). Retrieved October 15, 2018 from http://thelongcenter.org/2013/12/seinfeld-pat-hazell-talks-career-spanning-johnny-carson-wonder-bread-years-wonder-bread-years-december-19-22-long-center/

PART 3

Elements
The Dream Catcher Toolkit

6

Elements for Coaching

Biologically, the human body makes many of the nutrients that it needs to carry out its functions. Although called nonessential nutrients, they are, in fact, essential to health, as an excess or deficiency can lead to disease. There are another six nutrients: protein, carbohydrates, fats, vitamins, minerals, and water that the body can't make rapidly enough (or in some cases at all) to meet its daily needs. These are called essential nutrients and must be obtained from food or dietary supplements for the

> "SUCCESS IS NEITHER MAGICAL NOR MYSTERIOUS. SUCCESS IS THE NATURAL CONSEQUENCE OF CONSISTENTLY APPLYING THE BASIC FUNDAMENTALS."
>
> —Jim Rohn

continuing health of the body. According to the World Health Organization, a balanced diet is highly recommended so that the body receives all of the right nutrients for its specific needs.[1] Everyone's bodies are unique, thus different individuals require different amounts of these essential nutrients.

As with doctors and anyone else who understands the role nutrition plays in supporting a healthy body, a good coach knows that there are some

---

Dream Catcher, pages 53–80

key essential ingredients that their clients require to grow in their lives. Dream Catcher calls these "nutrients" **Elements**. Just as a nutritionist would look at an individual's needs by examining their specifications and biometrics, a coach must help analyze the needs of their client to find the right balance for using the Elements.

As a coach, you will learn to identify deficient Elements and guide your client towards a healthy and balanced diet. These Elements are the fundamental tool kit that you will apply to enable your client's success.

The following Elements are important tools because they are foundational and critical to the Dream Catcher coaching success. They are an access point to helping your client create a Compelling *Vision*, being able to *Execute* the steps towards that vision, and then having the ability to *Sustain* the journey to make the dream a firm reality. These three stages comprise the VES model—based on simple proven techniques designed to help you become a great coach and your client to achieve a successful outcome. We will look at the VES model and how the Elements support it in Part 4 of this book. First, we need to understand the Elements in detail.

Element #1: Authenticity

FACE IT UNTIL YOU MAKE IT

"BEING GENUINE IS THE FOUNDATION OF INTEGRITY— OFTEN INCONVENIENT AND NOT ALWAYS PAINLESS, BUT THE ONLY WAY TO GO IF YOU'RE HERE TO REALLY, TRULY, FULLY LIVE."

—Danielle Laporte

A few years ago, I met and got to know Joe, a successful business and family man. I enjoyed getting to learn from such a high achiever who was willing to share his free advice. Joe was something of a mentor for me and I really respected how open he was when we met. One day I asked him what were the biggest regrets he had and what were the failures he had learned from. I thought that he was going to share the usual clichés, but instead Joe told me that his biggest life lesson stemmed from him being a recovering alcoholic. From the age of 17 he had been a very heavy drinker.

He would black out, get into physical altercations, and make terrible decisions. His friends and family tried to intervene and offered to help him, but to no avail. The only "help" he received was that mandated by a judge. Joe said that for almost all of his early reckless life, his primary issue was that he told himself he had no problem. He drank heavily for 11 years with a further five years spent in several rehab programs, Alcoholics Anonymous (AA) meetings, and time with counselors. When he was not drinking, he put up a façade pretending that he was truly dealing with his alcohol problem.

Joe faked it—and almost didn't make it at all!

I asked him what had changed and how he had got and remained sober (for 18 years at the time of writing) and been able to turn his life around when many others fail. Joe reached into his pocket and pulled out a worn copper coin. As he handed it to me, he said, "This has been it for me." On it, a phrase was inscribed: "To Thine Own Self Be True."

It's a phrase originally from Shakespeare's play, *Hamlet.* That line is now etched on AA tokens and, for many who are in the program, carries a deep meaning. Joe told me that as an alcoholic predestined to die early as a drunk, every day he was sober was nothing short of miraculous. The advice on that token was the reminder Joe needed to either beat the urge to get a drink, or pick up the pieces after having relapsed. It kept him honest. "Whenever I relapsed, it felt as though the hope and confidence was drowned into obscurity with every swig I took from the bottle," Joe said. He continued to tell me that during his "dark years" he had thoughts of giving up. Life was meaningless. Joe told me "I would think to myself, why bother?

Hope is gone! It's replaced by guilt, shame, and anxiety." Even after 18 years of sobriety he spoke of his rough times as if they were just yesterday.

"Hi, My Name is Joe, and I'm an Alcoholic!"

The radical honesty required to follow AA's 12-step program typifies what it means to be true to yourself. To be able to look in the mirror and know you're being candid, genuine, and honest. After all, it's likely to have been a roller coaster of lies up until the day you really admit who you truly are.

In life and in business, we at times struggle with grasping a notion, understanding a concept, fitting in with others, and dealing with interpersonal issues. Some, like Joe, have been able to go through the most difficult of times and still achieve success. For others, life remains in constant turmoil—relationships, finances, work, the list is endless.

What differentiates these two types of people? In my opinion, it is trust. Trust is born from honesty. Trust leads to success! How then can people who struggle with the day-to-day problems of life trust themselves if they are not honest with themselves?

If success is correlated to being open and honest with oneself and being comfortable with the idea of one's vulnerability, then it is quite reasonable to predict that chaos, discontentment, and maybe depression are the likely outcomes for those that do not embrace and accept their true selves.

One of the most misleading pieces of advice I've ever heard is: "Fake it until you make it." Social psychologist and associate professor at Harvard Business School Amy Cuddy has a TED Talk with over six million views in which she discusses this.[2] She talks about body language and how it affects how others see us, but also how it may change how we see ourselves. Cuddy shows how "power posing," even when we don't feel inwardly confident, can raise confidence-boosting testosterone levels by up to 20% and decrease anxiety-causing cortisol levels in the brain. She posits that power posing likely has an impact on our chances for success. In essence, I would reframe the application of what Cuddy argues as a method for taking on the posture of someone you want to be perceived as. As a matter of fact it is a method we will discuss in the **Execution** chapter of this book.

The notion of "faking it," when diluted and misapplied, which it often is, derails and misapplies Cuddy's intentions and rationale. When offered as a prescription to someone who is most likely exhibiting behavior that engenders either a lack of confidence, competence, or courage, it can be very counterproductive.

Clearly, faking it until you make it could at times lead to the desired outcome. However, the side effects of this course of action may be even more serious than the initial malady of low confidence or skill that this remedy is attempting to cure.

When one is merely putting on a show and realizing short-term "success," is the result simply inflating your ego? This is not too dissimilar from having delusions of grandeur.

It is obviously not Cuddy's intent, but her advocacy of power posing may be misconstrued as support for insincerity, being disingenuous about our abilities, life situations, finances, and relationships, both professionally and personally.

By faking it, we endorse an approach that can become embedded in other aspects of our lives—something more than power posing and transcending more than body language. Such patterns of behavior can become dangerously cyclical. A pattern of inauthentic behavior could develop. When someone fakes it, they are avoiding confronting the really deep-rooted issues at hand and instead living life as a game of charades.

For example, maybe you know, or possibly you are, a person with low confidence in their leadership skills. This is probably accentuating your poor self-esteem, and may stem from a lack of knowledge. How helpful is it to put your efforts into acting/faking confidence and certainty in your leadership prowess? Rather, if you acknowledged that there is a gap between where you are and where you want to be as a leader you might make an investment into remedying the situation—learning more about how to truly develop yourself and grow into the person you want to be, someone with a legitimate and genuine healthy sense of self. You would, as a result, have far greater returns than by continuing to fake it.

Talent and ability cannot be developed if you pretend that you are already talented and capable. Faking it likely leads to inauthentic confidence and increased chronic anxiety arising from the fear of being discovered and exposed as deceitful, devious, and fraudulent.

Getting Your Client to Their Authentic Self

As a coach, your role is to help your client discover their genuine authentic self. If you are ever in doubt on how to guide your client and feel compelled to tell them to "Fake it until you make it"—Don't!

If your client mentions "faking it" as a strategy that they use, you should see this as a red flag, indicating upcoming turbulent times typified by floods of anxiety. If that is, or has been your client's approach, you must discern if there were or currently are insecurities, fears, and doubts that your client needs to face.

Help them rise above seeing themselves as a self-destructive fraudulent failure. If you really want to help them grow, do everything that you can to enhance their confidence and develop a constructive path forward.

Help them understand, appreciate, and learn to follow the maxim: "To Thine Own Self Be True."

Element #2: Bandwidth

TIME, ENERGY, AND EMOTIONS

Fact: We all have only 24 hours in a day. I have worked with a number of people who constantly leave me in awe; their voluminous workloads seem to have no impact on their tremendous productivity. These individuals have the rare ability to efficiently and seemingly effortlessly produce effective results. I have taken the time to look at and learn what makes these high producers tick. Despite what some people believe, I learned that these individuals aren't workaholics. They have managed to craft a lifestyle that allows them to do what others wish they had time for: exercise, get ample sleep, work hard and play just as hard. They

> "THE CAPACITY TO LEARN IS A GIFT; THE ABILITY TO LEARN IS A SKILL; THE WILLINGNESS TO LEARN IS A CHOICE."
>
> —Brian Herbert

seem to be able to take on and succeed at more than the average person. They have a higher and seemingly limitless capacity in so many regards. They have a wider bandwidth.

This insight has led to applying their principles, practices, and rituals to Dream Catcher's coaching model so that clients are able to harness the same 24 hours in a day we all have access to, and manage to be effective in everything we do.

Merriam-Webster defines bandwidth as *the emotional or mental capacity necessary to do or consider something.*[3]

The Element of bandwidth is vital in helping your clients be successful. Your client is going to need to learn and apply new skills, which means adding to an already heavy workload with commitments at work and in their personal life.

Adding more to the client's workload must be handled carefully. I have worked with people, including business leaders, some of whom are entrepreneurs who seem to be constantly drowning in work. They commit to working 12–14 hour days, seven days a week. Speaking to them, several had common experiences and thoughts. They shared complaints of constantly feeling exhausted and being constantly burdened by the guilt that they are missing out on other important things in their lives. It is clear that the physical, mental, and emotional toll on these people is damaging.

Dream Catcher is about learning, skill acquisition, and gap closure. Effective learning requires optimum conditions and having sufficient bandwidth. When looking at the lives of those individuals who are perpetually busy, it is clear that their bandwidth is limited. It is nearly impossible to effectively coach individuals who appear to be at the tipping point of falling apart because of other demands and commitments.

Learning, when reduced to its simplest form, is discovery. Coaching, when done correctly, is finding the right path to build skills that can help your client grow. If there are issues related to limited bandwidth, your client will fail dismally. Because of this, it is vital that all coaches understand the concept of bandwidth.

Adding more commitments to the already over-committed can only be done by stealing bandwidth from a limited resource. Those that grasp this know that bandwidth issues can threaten the acquisition of new skills. There are tools that your client must master in order to help them manage this issue during the coaching process.

Research has shown that time and energy are the main bandwidth issues that will affect client development.[4] Simply explained, time is the availability of hours during the day. Energy is categorized into two main parts: physical and emotional energy.

Understanding Time

The core problem with working long hours is that time is a finite resource. To be able to master it, it is important to establish key routines and rituals that allow space for the Dream Catcher process.

Master the To-Do List[5]

- Your client must utilize a to-do list.
- Understand how to approach the to-do list.
- Focus only on today.
- It may seem counterintuitive to productivity, but the shorter the list, the better.
- Place the bigger, more challenging, and most critical tasks for the day first. These are the things on the list that define success and failure on a day-to-day basis.
- Populate the rest of the list with items less critical to your success.
- Start the day by dealing with what is at the top of the list and work your way down.
- Don't put off critical things on the list to a later time; doing so is a recipe for failure.
- Only do the less important items on the list after the critical items are completed.

Understanding Energy

Assuming that your client already exhibits the authenticity element it will be easier for you to help them identify where their physical and emotional energy drains are. The main unnecessary drops in energy levels I have seen affect people are caused by an inability to balance workload with life's challenges. These are the people who tend to yearn for the idea of a "work–life balance."

When asked about work–life balance in 2006, Amazon CEO Jeff Bezos told Thrive Global about his preference for the word "harmony" over "balance" because the word balance tends to imply a strict tradeoff.[6] Just like many people I have worked with in organizations with a great culture, Bezos shared that if he was happy at work, it meant that he was a better person outside of work. The pleasure he experienced at work made him a better husband and father. This virtuous feedback loop also meant that if he was happy at home, he showed up to work "More energized…a better employee and a better colleague."

Dream Catcher subscribes to the idea of work–life harmony!

In the same interview, Bezos talked about the value of sleep and how he makes rest a priority. He shared that for him, sufficient rest helped him to keep high levels of energy and excitement. "Like many people in the world," Bezos said, "We don't need to maximize the number of decisions we make per day. Making a small number of key decisions well is more important than making a large number of decisions." Due to the sufficient rest he prioritizes, Bezos felt that he was more productive and efficient in terms of his decision-making. Moreover, his priority was on the quality of the decisions he made, not the quantity.

Most things in the Dream Catcher program involve behaviors and actions that clients must learn to do. Teaching clients rituals that will increase their energy and emotional bandwidth has proven difficult in most cases. In reality, as opposed to initiating certain actions, most clients actually need to learn to *stop* doing certain things.

Master Your Energy

- Stop taking on too much and not delegating others to handle issues.
- Stop handcuffing your team and its members.
- Stop being over-involved in areas that you don't need to.
- Stop making decisions that you don't have to make.
- Stop unnecessarily working "all-nighters."
- Stop saying yes to everything.
- Stop thinking you have to do everything by yourself.
- Stop refusing help.

Stopping these common behaviors will enable your client to increase their bandwidth exponentially. Your client will analyze where they are taking on unnecessary duties and look to delegate these to others who could take on some of that work. They will begin to ask for help so that they can have more time and space to dedicate to learning and skill acquisition.

Your client will learn when to say the word "No." They will learn to assess what are real priorities as opposed to favors that other team members ask them. They will be comfortable with not attending nonessential meetings and ignoring insignificant commitments that mean putting off the crucial things in their lives—such as their development.

Overall, the mastery of these common time and emotional drains will help your client in terms of their self-assurance. Your client will not measure success in terms of the time and effort spent on a project and how much midnight oil has been burnt. They will, instead, have trusted colleagues that they have developed and empowered to lighten their burden. Your client will begin to measure their results.

The power of bandwidth!

Element #3: Curiosity

ALWAYS BE CURIOUS (ABC)

> "CURIOSITY IS, IN GREAT AND GENEROUS MINDS, THE FIRST PASSION AND THE LAST."
>
> —Samuel Johnson

Growing up, I didn't learn much about Greek mythology and ancient Greek history. Despite my love of history and philosophy, I am probably one of the least qualified to speak on that subject. I did, however, enjoy my introduction to water displacement theory when I was a sixth grader.[7] It had nothing to do with the science behind the theory. It had more to do with the way the teacher explained the story to a group of 11-year-olds.

A grown man running around the streets of ancient Syracuse yelling "Eureka! Eureka!" Naked!

That was the entire story of Archimedes to me.[8]

In fact, the story is of a great mathematician, euphoric because of his great discovery. He had discovered the answer to a question that had been puzzling him for many years.

After ascending to the throne, King Hieron II of Syracuse, Sicily, had given a goldsmith a bar of gold to make into a crown. When he received his crown, Hieron suspected that the goldsmith had swindled him by removing some gold and replacing it with much cheaper silver. The only problem was that he couldn't prove his theory. Hieron asked Archimedes to establish, without damaging the crown, whether it was made from pure gold.

Archimedes told the king he would need a few days to think about the problem. He tried many methods and couldn't arrive at an answer. One day, while he was still pondering this conundrum, he took a bath in a tub full of water. When he got in the tub, he noticed that the water splashed out onto the floor the moment he stepped into it. As he sat down, even more water was displaced. Suddenly, he realized he had stumbled on the answer to the puzzle of the King's crown.

Archimedes had discovered that if he put the crown in water, it should displace the same amount of water as the amount of gold the King had given the goldsmith. It was not about weight. It was about density. Ultimately, the crown failed Archimedes' test. It was, indeed, not the king's gold. Eureka!

Dream Catcher, is about helping your client learn. Learning is about revelation and discovery and there can be no discovery without curiosity. The Element of curiosity is essential to help your client create a Compelling Vision, execute a plan to achieve it, and sustain the outcomes. Curiosity is also a quality that every coach should have.

Your client's dreams cannot be attained passively. Encourage them to be curious, proactive, and hungry for the necessary knowledge to attain the outcomes that they desire.

If a business doesn't care whether its team members are driven to learn then it is a rigid and mechanistic organization that isn't open to innovation and is destined to fail. The most agile businesses around the world actively encourage their people to fully exercise their curiosity.

Good coaches constantly ask their clients what they have been learning. At the same time, they ensure that they don't create an environment where their client looks to them for the answers. Superior coaches help their client seek the right answers through discovery.

As a coach, assess your interactions with your client. Make sure you are not creating a dependency in your client to seek the "right" answers from you, but rather empowering your client to seek truths for themselves. When you do this, your client and the organization that they work for will reap great benefits.

Benefits of Curiosity

Studies show that curiosity improves relationships. Work by some of the world's top psychology researchers—Dr. Todd Kashdan, Dr. Paul Rose, and Dr. Frank Fincham concluded that the degree to which people are curious influences their personal growth and the level of intimacy that develops when they meet someone new.[9] Dream Catcher requires deep relationships—both between the coach and the client and an extended network of advocates and supporters of the client to assist in skill building. Such connections also have benefits for an organization. Curiosity leads to the formation of new relationships that foster learning and self-discovery.

Another important benefit for your client and their organization is that curiosity stimulates and curious people have active brains. While the brain is not a muscle, just like a muscle, active brains improve with continual activity and exercise. Curious people grow.

Finally, curious people are more innovative. The degree to which your client is curious can directly affect their personal acumen as they learn more about themselves, their company, sector, and so on. Great companies are usually full of curious and innovative individuals.

Coaching Your Client to Develop Curiosity

Research by George Loewenstein, professor of economics and psychology in the Social and Decision Sciences Department at Carnegie Mellon University, and director of the Center for Behavioral Decision Research, shows that people are better at learning information when they are curious about the topic.[10] However, he theorizes that this is only the case if an individual has some initial knowledge on a subject. It is your role to facilitate acquiring initial knowledge on key subjects important for your client.

Here are a few fundamentals for you to practice as a coach and, in turn, help your client develop their curiosity prowess.

The Power of "I don't know"

- You must value learning more than appearing to be intelligent.
- Questions are vital. Ask questions that start with "how," "what," "when," "where," and "why."
- Be inquisitive. Encourage your client to get into the habit of asking others their opinions, perspectives, and their approaches to certain things.

It's Not About Me

- Seek to understand before you seek to be understood.
- It is OK to be wrong. Admitting this creates an environment where you are open to other people's thoughts and opinions.

Be Deliberate

- Schedule times to learn.
- Force yourself to try new methods; reinvent the wheel.
- Be attentive—and practice mindfulness.
- Answer the question, "What did I learn today that I didn't know before?"

Travel

- Be spontaneous and try new things: a route, a meal.
- Read literature, listen to music, do something that is out of your usual compass.
- Spend time to get to know someone different.
- Travel, literally.

Element #4: Support

PERSONAL BOARD OF ADVISORS (PBA)

How does a 23-year-old woman with zero experience in the food industry start a multimillion-dollar food business? Perhaps by borrowing a page out of the playbook that has led to the success of people like Oprah Winfrey, Jeff Bezos, and Elon Musk.

In an article in *Forbes*, Lisa Curtis shared the story of her success. She has a very impressive résumé.[11,12] She was named one of the *Forbes* "30 under 30" in the field of social entrepreneurship, worked for the Clinton Foundation, USAID, and also in the White House for the Obama administration. She also represented North American youth in the UN Environment Programme. While working for the Peace Corps in Niger she had the idea that led to her having a very successful business: Kuli Kuli, the company behind a green plant-based superfood called Moringa.[13]

Lisa took the path that Dream Catcher prescribes to all of those who believe that coaching will yield success. She looked to build an advisory board to help realize her business idea. She did this even before she had a business plan. Having a supportive network is essential to effective skill building and coaching.

Successful individuals often state that they seldom make important decisions in isolation. They rely on their advisors, a group of people that they trust to share their ideas and visions with and who can provide feedback and evaluation. They surround themselves with individuals who will help support the growth of their companies to reach new and greater heights.

With Dream Catcher it is important to look at whom your client has in their corner to consult with and seek advice from. It is also important for coaches to ask: "Who do I have as a coach in *my* life?" Support networks are important for both coaches and clients. Dream Catcher calls this support group your Personal Board of Advisors (PBA).

Because the PBA is an essential Element, it is important to evaluate the people your client has around them. Some may have a very healthy core group of advisors—friends, family, and colleagues. A few either won't have any or, worse, have toxic individuals close to them. People that may actually sabotage their success!

I have never had surgery, but I assume that, should I ever be in the situation to need a medic for any serious procedure, I would proceed with caution. Even if I weren't afforded the time to do my research, one of the questions I would ask is, "Who is the best qualified to perform this surgery?" The same applies when considering who should be on a PBA.

Dream Catcher has a method for assembling the right PBA. Because there are so many variables that must be taken into account when customizing any PBA, I will share a general summary of how to build one at the end of this section.

www.idreamidare.com members have access to the full resources available on the website to build a customized PBA.

The Ideal PBA

An effective PBA should include individuals who bring the following qualities:

- INSPIRATION: To gain insight and wisdom your client should include people that they have always looked up to or aspired to be like. Such people provide the inspiration typical of self-help books. These individuals will stimulate your client intellectually and act as catalysts for them to reach their dreams.

- ENLIGHTENMENT: If someone is curious, they constantly seek to learn. Having individuals on your board who are capable of feeding and guiding this zeal to learn through their willingness to shed light, clarity, knowledge, and wisdom is beneficial.

- MULTIPLICITY: There is value in having individuals on the PBA who are different from your client in terms of their perspective on life. Successful people benefit from spending time with others who see things through a different lens. A board with at least one member who has a very different outlook to your client is useful. This will create a diverse (non-groupthink) board. Diversity in intellect, background, age, race, politics, and other demographics all help. Amazing things happen when someone is exposed to and relishes having their eyes opened to different viewpoints.

- TRANSPARENCY: Having individuals who will honestly and transparently tell your client what they need to hear rather than what they want to hear is crucial. It is of paramount importance that your client has individuals who care enough to not be afraid to speak truthfully. If your client doesn't have someone who is able to cause temporary discomfort by being honest (even radically honest), challenging the status quo and provoking debate, then the coaching process may not be successful.

- LISTENING: It is important that the client has someone in their support group who, while not necessarily contributing directly by being creative or inspirational, understands and knows them well. Having someone they can turn to for a shoulder to lean on is a powerful thing. Just as the depth of your client's relationship with different friends will differ, it will also vary with their board. It is in the interest of your client to have someone who knows when to just listen and be there to pick them up when they are down.

If your client has people on their PBA to cover all of these needs you can rest easy as a coach. Experience shows that one person will do more than others. That person must be identified and should have more than one of the listed characteristics. If that is not the case, then someone new must be sought and added to the PBA.

Tips for Setting Up a PBA

Coaches, as well as their clients, should set up PBAs. It will help you develop both professionally and personally. Doing so will also make you more effective in helping your client develop a customized board.

The Right People in the Right Seats

In the next part of this book, you will learn how to create a Compelling Vision. Once created you must determine who you believe can help attain it. Look at the traits and experience of the people you have at your disposal and identify the people with the right qualities for your PBA. For example, once I had decided to commit to writing this book, one of the people I sought out for advice was a person who was already a published author.

Accessibility

The advisors on your board must be able to be reached easily. Yes, we all live in a digital world where Skype, instant messaging, and video conferencing is easy, however, a face-to-face relationship is vital. Local individuals are therefore ideal. Of course, you may have a person who you know is critical to your success in a distant location. Add them and make a commitment to connect as often as possible. Just make sure that they can also make the same commitment.

Preparation

If you have only a surface-level relationship with a potential advisor, be prepared to get to know them on a more meaningful level. Plan to begin your meeting with them with that end in mind. If you already know them well, be ready to clearly state what you would like from them. Have your Compelling Vision ready to present and explain what specific areas you believe they will add value to.

The Meeting

Your request to a potential PBA member should, whenever possible, be in person. Avoid email, as this is primarily for sharing information. Also avoid the telephone, as this is too impersonal. Telling someone face to face that you wish them to be involved in your self-improvement journey—that you respect them and would value their input into the process—is not only a big compliment, it is very difficult to decline. You are more likely to recruit your advisor in person. If they do decline, ask them if they can recommend or connect you with someone else that you could get to know. Someone with similar qualities.

What's in it for Them?

With preparation, you will be able to share what they may be able to get out of this relationship. I have often told my advisors that I do not have much to give them. However, I promise that I will work hard and will give them my commitment of time and follow-up. I also give them a platform where they can be as candid, open, and honest as they like. I also offer reciprocity—if they have anyone they feel that I can help as an advisor, I will do so. Of course, you should never make a promise that you cannot and will not keep.

Follow-Up

This can be done via email, though I prefer a handwritten note. Thank them for the meeting (whether or not they have agreed to join your PBA). Recap the conversation that you had and, if you have a follow-up scheduled, summarize the purpose and tell them you look forward to reconnecting.

Element #5: Practice

PRACTICE

PRACTICE

PRACTICE

DO WELL. DO OFTEN.

ANYTHING AND EVERYTHING
YOU PRACTICE, YOU'LL GET
GOOD AT.

K. Anders Ericsson, a psychologist and researcher at Florida State University co-authored a journal paper that he later expanded into a coauthored book called *Peak: Secrets from the New Science of Expertise.*[14, 15]

Ericsson wrote about two Hungarian educators from the 1970s: László and Klara Polgár. The two decided to challenge the popular assumption that women can't succeed in areas requiring spatial thinking, such as chess. The couple homeschooled their three daughters, who all learned and played chess with their parents. The systematic training and daily practice paid dividends. All three daughters, by the year 2000, had been ranked in the top ten female players in the world. The youngest, Judit, had become a grand master at the age of 15, breaking the previous record held by Bobby Fischer to become the youngest person to earn that ranking. Judit convincingly defeated almost all of the best male players she faced.

Ericsson also referenced the work of Benjamin Bloom, professor of education at the University of Chicago, who, in 1985, published a landmark book, *Developing Talent in Young People*, which examined the critical factors that contribute to the development of talent.[16] Bloom studied the childhoods of 120 elite performers who had won international competitions or awards in fields ranging from music and the arts to mathematics and neurology. Surprisingly, Bloom's work found no early childhood indicators that could have predicted the success of these elite performers. Further research in the field has also suggested that there is absolutely no correlation between IQ and expert performance in fields such as chess, music, sports, and medicine.[17]

Ericsson then pointed out a very interesting conclusion. The only innate differences that turn out to be significant for elite performance are physiological, such as height and body size—and these differences are only really relevant for sports!

With this science in mind, the Dream Catcher program believes that everyone is a coaching candidate for performance excellence as long as they meet the criteria spelled out in the earlier section on "Choosing the Right Client" [Part 2, p. 37]. It is safe to say that correlating innate ability and expert performance should be reserved for sports and other activities requiring physical prowess.

Ericsson (via Bloom's investigation) argued that the *only* corollary to success is that all superb performers had practiced intensively, had studied with devoted teachers, and had been supported enthusiastically by their families throughout their developing years. He also highlighted that subsequent research developed from Bloom's initial study revealed that the *amount* and *quality* of practice were key factors in the level of expertise people achieved. Through verifiable science and a reproducible methodology, Ericsson proved that "consistently and overwhelmingly, the evidence showed that experts are always made, not born."

The expert performers that Ericsson studied came from a wide variety of disciplines: surgeons, actors, chess grandmasters, writers, computer programmers, musicians, and many others.

To the preceding list of disciplines I will add coaching. You can be a highly skilled coach as long as you follow the guidance of good teachers and practice your craft. Dream Catcher is a program that can assist you with that journey. Moreover, by adopting the key principles, those you coach will yield significant results.

Practice Makes Excellence

Trev Alberts is a name very familiar to Nebraska natives.[18] The University of Nebraska Omaha (UNO) appointed him vice chancellor after he had previously been the athletics director. Under his leadership, UNO athletics moved up to the esteemed Division I. He is, however, more renowned for

> "MY DAD ALWAYS TOLD US, SET YOUR GOALS WAY UP THERE. TRY YOUR BEST. IF YOU MISS THE MARK A LITTLE BIT, YOU ARE WAY HIGHER THAN YOU EVER WERE BEFORE."
>
> —Trev Alberts

his time as an athlete, playing football at the University of Nebraska-Lincoln. Not many defensive players in the school's history are more decorated than Trev, who became the Huskers' first Butkus Award winner in 1993. It was a championship year for the program.

Trev also knows quite a lot about the application of deliberate practice as he has done much of this both in sports and business. Speaking with Trev, it quickly becomes clear that he has a big vision and lofty goals. Whether it's at work or in his personal life, he is driven. "I need goals. I need to be fighting for something," he stresses. This has served him well across his life, playing for Coach Tom Osbourne, as a college football commentator on ESPN, and being a great father.[19]

Trev shared that he had never had any coaching to become a broadcaster and taking on such a role was both humbling and completely outside of his comfort zone. He did, however, do what he had always done to succeed, work hard and practice intensively. The same applied when he took on the job at UNO as athletics director. He had previously more or less only worked for himself; "I had never led an organization." It was time for him to learn new skills. He worked hard to learn the business side. He jokingly told me that one of the most intimidating things he faced during his early days was chairing meetings with staff, head coaches, executives, and student athletes. It didn't matter that he had played at the highest levels of the NFL; these were unfamiliar skills that he now had to learn. He applied himself to the task of deliberate practice to master the skill of meeting facilitation.

When I asked about his approach and how he quickened his learning process, Trev told me, "There are no shortcuts. You simply have to focus on doing things the right way in order to succeed." He reminisced about his time spent with Coach Osbourne: "We did the same thing over and over. Routine was part of our lives. Coach instilled habits that we had to execute in the right way."

Just as Coach Osbourne provided a practice routine for Trev, as a coach you hold the key to finding your own practice methods to unlock the potential for others to attain expert performance.

- ▪ INTENSIVE PRACTICE: When your client signs a contract with you stating that they will work hard, it is worth reiterating to them you are going to be doing the same. Coach Osbourne didn't only set work for Trev and his teammates; he also had his part to do. He had to make sure that the routines that his team spent long hours practicing would be applied on the playing field on game day and perhaps also later in life.

- DEVOTED TEACHER: You will care about and be committed to the success of your client. That's a key element of being a Dream Catcher coach. You will be prepared for meetings and do your part to help your client. You will help guide them and operate within the ethos recommended by the program. Whenever you are unable to assist your client, you will be transparent about your limitations and seek whatever additional help is needed to serve them.

- AMOUNT AND QUALITY OF PRACTICE: It's your client's responsibility to put in the time and effort to stretch their capabilities. It is your role to help them design appropriate practice sessions that are aligned with their Compelling Vision. You need to do your research to ensure that you can define what this may be comprised of. This means that you will need to utilize the Dream Catcher Elements and apply them to yourself as a coach. It also requires you to hone your craft, using additional resources such as those that can be accessed on **www.idreamidare.com**.

Trev Alberts left me with some important insights on the idea of deliberate practice. From the time he was a young man, he had the support that Professor Ericsson believes is essential to expert performance. Trev's father made sure that whatever his son did was practiced intensively and to the best of his ability. His father was a devoted teacher and instilled the lesson of the quality of practice.

Not everyone has had that in life. Perhaps some individuals that we coach have obstacles that they need to overcome. They may have developed bad habits and routines in the past. It is quite possible that they have become experts while retaining bad habits. You will need to prepare for these possibilities with your client. I have worked with people who have done extremely well in overcoming their bad habits. However, when they are either facing stressful situations or aren't as mindful as usual, the old habits can creep back in. This is something that you should listen out for when your client shares their Compelling Vision and the obstacles they face in attaining it.

Deliberate Practice Worksheet

DREAM
CATCHER

1. BEGIN WITH A DISTINCT AND SPECIFIC FOCUS AREA

Always review the 3-year Compelling Vision (CV). This is where you will identify the 1-3 focus areas to work on. With your client use the CV to narrow down and define the exact and precise focus area(s). Follow a 'What-Definition-How' process.

Example: "I want to be a more effective leader." Define what that means and what it would take. "That means that I need to focus on the people I lead by listening more and communicating effectively." What practical steps can you take to develop these skills? "To achieve this, I have to practice speaking less and apply the technique 'W.A.I.T: Why Am I Talking'.

Begin with the end in mind and work towards a specific outcome. What is the CV? What is the necessary work required to make measureable progress towards attaining this vision?

2. ALWAYS REMEMBER THE COMPELLING VISION

Deliberate practice is a commitment that requires determination, perseverance, and the participant's fullest attention for the 12-plus week session.

Example: This week, I will read the book, Never Split the Difference: Negotiating As If Your Life Depended On It. I will break down and list the skills that I am lacking in my approach to communication. I will review them with my coach and focus on the steps I need to take to improve. We will develop a plan next week on how to diligently involve my team members in the application of the plan.

Define a specific short-term commitment towards making progress towards the 3-year Compelling Vision. Agree on the duration, amount and quality of practice that will be involved.

3. REVIEW

What is going well? What is being done correctly and incorrectly? These are important questions to answer. This information will come from different sources—team members, coach observation, and especially from journaling, self-reflection, and introspection. Encourage authenticity.

4. SUCCESS RESIDES OUTSIDE OF YOUR COMFORT ZONE.

New things that will stretch your client are vital. Move your client out of their comfort zone to try novel things to help development. They may run into challenges. As a coach you must guide your client.

Example: "Go and negotiate a purchase this week. Apply the steps from the book that require listening and then speaking effectively in order to get the other party to accept your negotiation"

Each week ask what unique and uncomfortable steps they will take to develop their skills.

Read Dr. Anders Ericsson's book, Peak: Secrets From the New Science of Expertise for deeper understanding of the concept of deliberate practice.

Dream Dare Do!

This worksheet and other resources can also be found on **www .idreamidare.com**. Visit the site to access it or to request a copy.

Element #6: Review

A RAISED SENSE OF SELF-AWARENESS

Jon is one of the most talented people I know. He is a self-taught blues harmonica player, an accomplished photographer, and an amazing story-teller.[20] He is also QLI's director of creativity and a certified Dream Catcher coach. Jon was coaching a young woman at QLI and had some pertinent experience with one of the key Elements that makes Dream Catcher effective.

Clinical teams meet regularly to develop care and treatment plans for the people who have entrusted QLI to help rebuild their lives. In these sessions it is very important that the team understand each client's individual needs. Jon's client was involved in such a team and so he decided to attend a meeting to observe and review her performance and suggest areas for growth.

It sounds simple. It's not!

Jon's client was Taylor, one of the most respected leaders at QLI. As the director of clinical services, her role included leading a team of speech and language pathologists who work across the company, as well as collaborating with various teams across the organization to help create the unique fortified multidisciplinary program characterized by across-the-board expertise. Taylor is the recipient of QLI's prestigious James P. O'Donnell Demonstrated Excellence Award, which is bestowed on those who exemplify the extremely high standards of excellence demanded of all at QLI. Her knowledge has helped shape the programs at QLI and has contributed to making the services of the highest possible quality, allowing QLI to be a reputable national center of excellence.

Taylor invited Jon to observe her in the meeting she was facilitating with her team. Before they started, Jon and Taylor let the team know that he was there to observe in order to help her improve her effectiveness as a facilitator and that they would later review her performance.

After the meeting it was clear that the team was intrigued with what form the review process would take and someone asked if they could observe the process. Soon, the entire rehabilitation team also wanted to observe. Taylor and Jon saw an opportunity to be role models and happily obliged. Jon broke down her performance, citing some areas that she could improve on. Taylor shared why some of these issues existed. For example, if Taylor knew that there was an issue that a specific therapist should take on, she would ask, "Who wants to own that?" Taylor said that this was because she wasn't comfortable with the idea of directing or ordering what someone should do. The team, observing the process, said that they would prefer it if Taylor directed them as they trusted and welcomed her opinion.

The outcome of the review process not only gave Taylor greater awareness of how her team felt, it also led to the team becoming conscious of their leader's desire to develop in particular areas. To this day, the team continues to support their boss, who is now also a Dream Catcher coach, when her old habits creep back in. The team appreciates it when she is open and direct with them and they feel able to reciprocate with her.

There are many people at QLI that have been inspired to seek out coaching because of Taylor and Jon's transparent process and this has helped to perpetuate the coaching culture within the company. Many team members didn't see Taylor's process with Jon as something expected by management. Rather, it was seen as being an inspirational example of how QLI empowered its employees and led them to become more comfortable with being coached.

This example highlights the importance of the Dream Catcher Element, "Review." It's a process similar to something used by many sports coaches.

For example, NFL players start the week by reviewing film of their previous game. The coaches take the opportunity to identify mistakes and correct them, both individually and as a unit. In an article he wrote for *Bleacher Report*, Marc Lillibridge, a former scout for the Green Bay Packers and Kansas City Chiefs, gave insight on this practice.[21] He stated that it is used to highlight both good and bad elements: bad positioning, correct techniques, successful plays, and so on. Players such as Peyton Manning and Larry Fitzgerald have commented that they have a voracious appetite for reviewing their performance as they believe it enhances their skill levels. The review process is not only used for looking at things retroactively and moving on; teams also use film to prepare for their next opponent.

As we attempt to improve and succeed in life and business, the main opponent we face is often ourself. The purpose of reviewing how we performed a particular task or dealt with an interaction is to improve how we do it next time. By closing gaps and building skills that lead to expert performance we are taking the right steps to get closer to our Compelling Vision.

Aside from observation and feedback, Dream Catcher uses other review tools and techniques that you and your client will benefit from. Some of these include journaling, mindfulness practice, and utilizing accountability groups; all things that Taylor and others practice.

One of the most useful methods of Review is the practice of journaling. It is important that every Dream Catcher coach emphasize the practice of independent self-analysis so that their clients learn how to self-assess and evaluate their endeavors.

Journaling

Journaling—writing down thoughts and feelings—is a tool that will benefit both you and your client in important ways. It is a modality that can be applied to many aspects of your client's life, and will enable them to elaborate on where they currently are in relation to where they want to be. By honestly and authentically reflecting on performance, areas for improvement become clear.

I encourage journaling by handing out a physical journal to my clients when we begin our coaching process. I encourage all of my clients to unplug and journal in a distraction-free environment. Because journaling is a very versatile tool, there are a number of benefits from the practice, including:

- TRUTH: Clients tend to be more unfiltered when writing things down and they find the practice to be nonjudgmental.
- PRESENCE: When done well, journaling is about being present in the moment and allows for reflection.
- CLARITY: Clients have been able to write their clear and refined thoughts when journaling. They have also been able to break down and organize those thoughts.
- NOVELTY: Journaling has helped Dream Catcher clients to deepen their thoughts and explore their implications leading to new self-discovery.
- MENTAL MAPPING: When they have practiced journaling, clients have been able to make new connections about their lives that

are amazing. This is one of the many reasons why clinical psychologists recommend journaling.[22]

▪ HISTORICAL ACCOUNT: Another great benefit for journaling is that it serves as a record of progress for your client. As it evolves, the journal helps document the client's development process.

All of these resources can be explored further by visiting Dream Catcher's website, **www.idreamidare.com**.

Finally, as a coach, you will spend as much time as you can with your client not only reviewing their performance, but also their Compelling Vision—the ultimate destination that helps keep their sights locked in on their ideal future while simultaneously having a firm grip on their life today.

SUMMARY

The six Elements are a tool kit for coaches to use with a client. When used in combination, they are as essential to the development of your client as a balanced diet is to the human body. The Elements are not solely indigenous to either personal or business life; they are applicable to all aspects.

As a Dream Catcher coach you must add these to your repertoire of knowledge and it is highly recommended that they are also applied to the coach's daily practice. This will increase the effectiveness of your knowledge as a coach, thus promoting your clients to develop skills, close gaps, grow, and in turn, help your organization's mission.

You will know when it is time to adjust the mix of how the Elements are used as the relationship develops.

The Elements that should be applied to all three areas of the coaching model are:

▪ **Authenticity**: Face it until you make it. To thine own self, be true.
▪ **Bandwidth**: We all have a fixed amount of resources in our lives. There is also only so much that a person can accommodate. Always weigh up with your client what they are capable of taking on. Be realistic.
▪ **Curiosity**: Always be curious. If your client isn't learning, the process isn't working.
▪ **Support**: A PBA is vital for both you and your client. Everyone needs the right people around them—people who will encourage, support and stretch you, and be instrumental to growth.

- **Practice**: You become good at what you do often. It is imperative to deliberately practice behavior that will lead to success.
- **Review**: By observing performance and offering feedback you can provide your client with valuable feedback on how to improve. Journaling assists self-reflection.

Practicing the Elements is helpful to client development. Coaches using these tools have found great success not only in being able to relate better to their clients, but also by being able to implement the process in their own lives.

Notes

1. Nutrients. (2017, December 19). Retrieved September 8, 2018 from http://www.who.int/elena/nutrient/en/
2. Cuddy, A. (n.d.). Your body language may shape who you are. Retrieved from https://www.ted.com/talks/amy_cuddy_your_body_language_shapes_who_you_are?language=en
3. Bandwidth. (n.d.). Retrieved October 20, 2018 from https://www.merriam-webster.com/dictionary/bandwidth?utm_campaign=sd&utm_medium=serp&utm_source=jsonld
4. Ormrod, J. E. (2017). Bringing other factors into the picture: How emotions, dispositions, and attributions affect thinking and learning. In J. E. Ormrod, *How we think and learn: Theoretical perspectives and practical implications* (pp. 145–160). Cambridge, England: Cambridge University Press.
5. Schrager, S., & Sadowski, E. (2016). Getting more done: Strategies to increase scholarly productivity. *A Journal of Graduate Medical Education, 8*(1), 10–13.
6. Thrive Global. (2016, November 30). Jeff Bezos: Why getting 8 hours of sleep is good for Amazon shareholders. Retrieved from https://medium.com/thrive-global/jeff-bezos-sleep-amazon-19c617c59daa
7. Britannica, T. (2017, December 13). Archimedes' principle. Retrieved from https://www.britannica.com/science/Archimedes-principle
8. Archimedes. (n.d.). Retrieved October 20, 2018 from http://www.ancientgreece.com/s/People/Archimedes/
9. Kashdan, T. B., Rose, P., & Fincham, F. D. (2004). Curiosity and exploration: Facilitating positive subjective experiences and personal growth opportunities. *Journal of Personality Assessment, 82*(3), 291–305.
10. Loewenstein, G. (1994). The psychology of curiosity: A review and reinterpretation. *Psychological Bulletin, 116*(1), 75–98.
11. Curtis, L. (2018, May 26). *Why you need an advisory board before a business plan.* Retrieved from https://www.forbes.com/sites/lisacurtis/2018/05/26/why-you-need-an-advisory-board-before-a-business-plan/#201d8bf92f95
12. Kuli Kuli. (n.d.). Retrieved from https://www.kulikulifoods.com/about

13. Moringa: Uses, side effects, interactions, dosage, and warning. (n.d.). Retrieved from https://www.webmd.com/vitamins/ai/ingredientmono-1242/moringa

14. Ericsson, K. A., Krampe, R. T., & Tesch-Romer, C. (1993). The role of deliberate practice in the acquisition of expert performance. *Psychological Review, 100*(3), 363–406. http://dx.doi.org/10.1037/0033-295X.89.4.369

15. Ericsson, A., & Pool, R. (2017). *Peak: Secrets from the new science of expertise.* Boston, MA: Mariner Books.

16. Bloom, B. (n.d.). Developing talent in young people. Retrieved from https://www.penguinrandomhouse.com/books/15009/developing-talent-in-young-people-by-dr-benjamin-bloom/9780345315090

17. Ericsson, K. A., & Charness, N. (1994). Expert performance: Its structure and acquisition. *American Psychologist, 49*(8), 725–747.

18. Trev Alberts. (n.d.). Retrieved from https://www.unomaha.edu/about-uno/administration-profiles/trev-alberts.php

19. http://coachtomosborne.com

20. Pearson, J. (n.d.). Jon Pearson. Retrieved September 08, 2018, from https://www.streetbeatphoto.com/

21. Lillibridge, M. (2017, October 03). A Former Player's Perspective on Film Study and Preparing for an NFL Game. Retrieved August 27, 2018 from https://syndication.bleacherreport.com/amp/1427449-a-former-players-perspective-on-film-study-and-preparing-for-a-nfl-game.amp.html

22. Journaling in Therapy. (n.d.). Retrieved from https://www.psychologytoday.com/us/blog/in-therapy/201101/journaling-in-therapy

7

Think, Talk, and Act Like a Coach

There is a huge difference between monologue and dialogue. As a coach, if you ever find yourself speaking much more than your client, you are likely in danger of delivering a monologue. You cannot coach by "telling." It is not the coach's job to hand a client the answers and solutions to their questions. A Dream Catcher coach is there to guide their client towards their own solutions, and hold them accountable for taking the necessary action.

> GREAT TEACHERS GIVE YOU A GLIMPSE OF THE WORLD YOU'VE NEVER IMAGINED.
>
> THE EXCEPTIONAL TEACHER LEAVES YOU BELIEVING THAT YOU CAN RULE THAT WORLD!
>
> —Tinashe Mahupete

Rich Dialogue

Effective communication is a constant problem in businesses around the world. When I have asked business leaders for one thing they feel can improve in their company, communication is invariably in the top five responses. It should be quite alarming that this continues to plague businesses and perhaps society in general when it is something we spend a significant amount of time doing via face-to-face meetings, emails, texts, video conferencing, and social network programs. Information is being exchanged constantly, but who is truly paying attention? The problem seems to be a lack of attention and even more so, a lack of willingness to understand. When values and beliefs differ, a lack of effective communication can actually create strife and arguments. This should be disturbing for us as a society as we continue to migrate into more impersonal modes of communication.

Being a good communicator is a skill that should be valued very highly. Being able to facilitate dialogue, engage in conversation, and extract meaning from content are essential skills in all aspects of life.

Facilitating rich dialogue is critical to the process of coaching. It is imperative to develop skills that foster a cooperative dialogue between individuals to stimulate critical thinking and to draw out ideas and underlying assumptions. I mentioned earlier my love for classical Greek stories and figures. One of my favorites regards the philosopher Socrates. Socrates was a master of examining the unexamined through pointed, insightful questions.

Perhaps by practicing how to ask probing questions, uncover preconceptions, deconstruct thoughts and ideas, find the outliers, and seek to understand others, we will improve our world. For the moment we will take the necessary steps towards that as a small group of people—Dream Catchers.

30%
DREAM CATCHER COACH

70% CLIENT

THE SWEET SPOT of DIALOGUE

For the Strong and Silent Type

Early on in my career at QLI, I was the quiet type who was more comfortable with silence. This was partly because I was trying to fit into a new country and culture, but also because I was self-conscious about my accent. I was, and still am, a very private person and so I didn't easily share my personal thoughts or feelings. To this day my wife enjoys spending time with my sisters because she jokingly says that she has gotten to know me through them! Still, I wanted to grow as a leader and in order to do that my silence was certainly not golden. Relationships are the lodestar of how QLI works as an organization and my reticence was a barrier to my success. QLI's founder, Dr. Kim Hoogeveen, taught me that I could capitalize on my silence and at the same time be the more social person I wanted to be. "The person who speaks the most believes the conversation went the best," Kim asserted. I just had to improve my skills at enabling others to talk. I started with team members, residents, families, and people outside of work. It seemed simple: ask the right questions and listen and people would talk about an array of subjects. After taking tours of QLI's facilities with families, they would at times comment on how personable I was. I developed a reputation as a person who was skilled at building relationships and knew more about people than other team members; yet I remained a rather mysterious person who others knew very little about. The best Dream Catcher coaches are those who have learned how to really get to know the people around them. For those who are naturally more private, I am an example that they can also coach well. There are other more outgoing and vocal coaches who have had to learn the art of being more reserved and open to listening.

The Social Bee

Everyone can be an effective coach if they know how to create an environment where their client will speak up and be open. As a more reserved individual, such "social bees" are my favorite type of people. For example, I have really enjoyed working with Jenn during my time at QLI. She made a very fast ascent at the company and became known as a very effective supervisor with great ability to create actionable steps from well thought out ideas. Many of the residents who come to QLI have their heads hanging, defeated by the belief that, because of their injuries, their lives are now worthless. People like Jenn can turn defeatism around and create positivity and hope. She has the ability to help them see that it's not the end of the story but the beginning of a new chapter.

A skill that Jenn had to learn in order to become a more effective leader was slowing down her natural vivacity and listening more. One of the tools she was introduced to was a system called W.A.I.T. (Why Am I Talking).[1]

Jenn worked with this tool and has become a very effective leader who gets to really know the team members she manages and leads but leaves them space to talk as she listens. She has the awareness and commitment to speak purposely and deliberately, at the right time.

If you become aware that you tend to share *too* much and that could affect your role as a coach ask yourself to W.A.I.T. Some of the reasons people speak too much may include:

1. I want to deliberately and purposely communicate.
2. I have an urge to share.
3. Everyone else is talking.
4. I want attention.
5. Your story reminds me of mine.
6. I don't know why I am talking.

Unless you are communicating deliberately and purposely, it is paramount to practice the W.A.I.T technique.

It's Not an Interrogation

For a coach to become an effective communicator they must have the ability to facilitate their client opening up. They must also be able to listen and understand what the client is communicating to them.

> "THE ART AND SCIENCE OF ASKING QUESTIONS IS THE SOURCE OF ALL KNOWLEDGE."
>
> —Thomas Berger

This is a challenging skill to master if what you are hearing clashes with your personal views, beliefs, and values. It is important to enter coaching sessions with the mindset that you are not there to judge. This doesn't mean you cannot ask questions. When faced with a conflict in terms of views and values, remember to refer back to the importance of rich dialogue. In any case, whether or not you endorse or question your client's beliefs, a good Dream Catcher coach consistently focuses on how they ask questions in a non-interrogatory manner.

I have partnered with and invited supervisors, supporters, and other people who the client was comfortable with to join me in some coaching sessions. This has either been for the benefit of the client, or when I have wanted some help as a coach. When it has been for my benefit, I have reviewed my performance with the observers. The feedback has often focused on how I repeatedly asked the question "Why?" and how the client was comfortable in sharing each time I asked that question.

There is an element of truth in this. "Why" is important, but there is also a skill and method in how you should ask questions of your client. Provocative queries that will lead to creating a great level of discomfort should be avoided. Instead you should help your client to explain the perspective that they have and carefully reveal what this may mean.

When I recapped with my observers the actual questions that I had asked my client, they got a deeper understanding of the process. There were particular questions I asked that helped my client lead us to an understanding of the "Why." As a prospective coach, I challenge you to practice asking "Why" questions without using that actual word.

Moreover, what my observers later discovered was that there were times my client divulged the answer to why, without a question even being asked. These are strategies that you will learn in the next section of this book as you help your client create a vision. First, we will cover the basics.

Positive Questions for Your Client

- What's the update on...?
- What can I do to be helpful to you?
- Given that was the outcome, how would you do it differently next time?
- How are you feeling about...?
- How are your emotions affecting or influencing your perception?
- Can you tell me a bit more about that mistake you made?
- Could you help me understand by walking me through your process?
- Can you elaborate further on what you mean by that?

ASK YOURSELF: "Is the nature of my question promoting dialogue or stopping the conversation?"

Remember, only the inquisitive mind solves problems.

Wean Them Off GPS

The Dream Catcher process is about the long-term acquisition of skills and knowledge. It's like being in a new city and trying to find your way around. You could use your phone's GPS directions to get to your destination with the dictated turn-by-turn instructions. Sure, you will get "there," but you'll never really learn the route. You still won't know how the city is really laid out. You will come to rely on the GPS. Without it, you cannot reliably take a simple drive to a point of interest, despite the fact that you've been there numerous times before. The Dream Catcher coach does not give into the temptation to provide a GPS route—quick answers and shortcuts that will lead their client to continue to rely on them. The ideal coach works hard to listen to questions, think about the end goal, and help their client develop their own self-navigation skills wherever possible. Help your client find their inner compass.

Be 100% Committed

The ideal traits of a coach have already been covered. However, there is a big difference between possessing the right traits and living them. There are numerous times when people with great characters fall short. It is vital that every interaction with your client reflects key truths. Your client must believe that you are 100% committed to the process, unquestionably. Some of these key truths are:

I Genuinely Value You

- It's not about me!
- This is not an acquired skill or an emotionally driven characteristic.
- It's an act of the will. Devotion (allegiance), not emotion!

I Believe in Your Goals, Ambitions, and Potential

- If I don't share belief in your goals, it is a coaching mismatch.
- Be truthful. Never fake it.
- I am all in on creating an honest relationship and understanding why you value what you value.
- I will invest my time, energy, and network to align with your ambitions.

I Am Committed to Your Success.

- My time with you is sacred.
- I don't turn it off. I am constantly thinking about you and seeking resources to assist you.
- I listen to and hear what you are saying.
- My commitment to you overrides any personal agenda.

From Vulnerability to Trust

The responsibility for creating trust lies with the coach. Without trust, your grasp on the Elements, comprehending the Vision of your client, and being well qualified to help them succeed is useless.

If your relationship with your client is based on trust, they will be more apt to develop confidence and have faith in the process. More specifically, they will trust in your ability as a coach. Your client will not have fear and be willing to be open, both with you and with their feelings.

As a coach, the aim is to work hard to build trust with your client. Where a client would typically feel vulnerable, you must appreciate the need to facilitate a relationship where the client is confident in you. By acknowledging that the coaching process is not about you, but about your client, you will understand that it is your responsibility to foster a safe environment—free of judgement and full of truth! Building trust is essential in unlocking the potential within others and helping them to close The Gap and move outside of their comfort zones. If a client tells you that they feel vulnerable during a session, reassure them by saying: "You were trusting of me and I appreciate that."

> "IF I CAN LISTEN TO WHAT HE CAN TELL ME, IF I CAN UNDERSTAND HOW IT SEEMS TO HIM; IF I CAN SEE ITS PERSONAL MEANING FOR HIM, IF I CAN SENSE THE EMOTIONAL FLAVOR WHICH IT HAS FOR HIM, THEN I WILL BE RELEASING POTENT FORCES OF CHANGE IN HIM."
>
> —Carl Rogers

The Dream Catcher Timeline

3-Year Vision

For your client, it all starts with their Compelling Vision—a clear and bright picture of their ideal self. As a coach, you will be equipped to help your client work through the process of creating this Compelling Vision for their future.

Unlike other programs that may take people between five and ten years to complete and can be quite fuzzy, Dream Catcher looks to reduce the coaching time to just three years, which, from my experience, is both more tangible and eminently achievable. If you ask someone to dream big on a ten-year time horizon, the tangibility of the aspiration can seem less clear. Conversely, if we try to achieve big dreams in too short a time—a year, say— the ambition of the dream would need to be scaled back. Three years is the right length of time for Dream Catcher.

It is important to understand that throughout the process, the Compelling Vision of your client could evolve. That is actually a good thing. The process envisages going as far as the mind's eye can see. As the journey takes your client closer to their destination, they may be able to see further.

The 12-Week Session

It has been stated that it takes just 21 days to create a habit. That is actually completely false and has now been debunked. Research led by a team at University College London has come closer to uncovering how long (on average) it takes for a behavior to become habitual.[2] They believe that it takes an average of 66 days to create a habit. Dream Catcher subscribes to the idea of habit formation as a key factor in its coaching methods. It is because of this that I believe that a period of *at least* 12 weeks be set aside to address gap closure and identifying the skill building that will eventually lead to mastery. During this period, I recommend meeting with your client at least twice a week for at least 30–45 minutes. In my experience, a meeting at the beginning and at the end of the working week is ideal. These meetings serve the purpose of setting up and then deliberating on how the week has gone. There is also a dashboard for communication between the coach and client that subscribing coaches can utilize at **www.idreamidare.com**.

Focus Areas

Focus is a very important part of the coaching program. Bandwidth is always affected when people have more things added to their workload. This coaching program is intense and calls for complete commitment in order to be successful. Because of this, I highly recommend focusing on just one area at a time. There have been exceptions made to this rule. For example, QLI has a unique leadership apprentice program. It is program to which people apply and then go through a rigorous selection process. If successful they have a 12-month period in which they are assigned a coach and follow a curriculum that is designed to help them develop as a leader. The Dream Catcher program is a part of this process and because the aim is the rapid development of future leaders, up to three focus areas are allowed. However, in typical situations, because every client likely has other life obligations, just one focus area should be targeted. If your client wants more, slow them down and insist that you work together on a manageable and productive process.

SUMMARY

Think like a coach:

- The Dream Catcher coach genuinely values their client.
- They believe in their client's goals, ambitions, and potential.
- They believe that the coaching process requires implicit trust.

Act like a coach:

- Coaches must learn and exercise the practice of listening intently to understand their client.
- An effective coach adapts their style to help different types of clients.
- Coaches are committed to their client's success.

Talk like a coach:

- Dialogue is essential for the Dream Catcher process to be effective.
- The coach's role is to help guide the client to revealing answers, not telling them what to do.
- Only the inquisitive mind solves problems. There are methods of finding the answer to "Why" without directly asking the question.

Dream Catcher Timeline:

- 3-year Compelling Vision (as far as the mind can see).
- 12-week (minimum) sessions.
- Ideally focus on only one area for skill development, with no more than three focus areas in rare circumstances.

Notes

1. W.A.I.T.—Why Am I Talking? (n.d.). Retrieved October 21, 2018 from https://powerofted.com/w-a-i-t-why-am-i-talking/
2. Lally, P., Jaarsveld, C. H., Potts, H. W., & Wardle, J. (2009). How are habits formed: Modelling habit formation in the real world. *European Journal of Social Psychology, 40*(6), 998–1009.

$$8$$

Vision

A vision is a vivid mental picture of an ideal future. Dream Catcher operates on the strength of your client's vision—which I will refer to from here on out as the Compelling Vision. Ultimately, your client's Compelling Vision must be so powerful that it can serve as a continual road map for their success. Any person who starts their journey with a clear vision will be undeterred by temporary set-

> "THE BEST WAY TO PREDICT THE FUTURE IS TO CREATE IT."
>
> —Abraham Lincoln

backs. The vision becomes a foundational intrinsic force so powerful that your client will have the zeal to pursue their desired future in spite of any obstacles.

The Purpose of a Vision

The Compelling Vision of your client can and should change over time. It's a process of evolution. It's progressive. Experiencing and attaining goals along the path of this process will cause this to happen. As goals are

Dream Catcher, pages 93–99
Copyright © 2019 by Information Age Publishing
93

achieved, things become clearer and thus should lead to changes in regard to what direction you decide to take going forward.

> "IF YOU AIM AT NOTHING, YOU WILL HIT IT EVERY TIME."
>
> —Zig Ziglar

The Compelling Vision is a blueprint for life. Blueprints aren't vague and void of detail and specifics. If they were, it would be impossible to construct something real from them. The unique part of the Dream Catcher blueprint is that it is meant to evolve, to develop along with your client through the process. Knowing the purpose of the Compelling Vision is essential for both the coach and client. Dream Catcher has synthesized the many purposes and benefits of a Compelling Vision for the coach and client to remember and apply. The compelling vision will galvanize your client in times when they need to focus, to insist, to strengthen, and to hope (FISH).

FOCUS: Kouzes and Ponser defined vision as, "an ideal and unique image of the future."[1] Going into the 1996 Olympics, 18-year-old U.S. gymnast Kerri Strug envisioned winning the gold medal. Strug was the final gymnast on the vault and the title was on the line. On her first attempt, she fell and tore ligaments in her left ankle. She had one final attempt to secure the gold. Limping, and in pain, it seemed that all was lost. Even today, it is riveting to watch the video of Strug sprinting for her final vault attempt, and landing it perfectly—on one leg—saluting the judges, and finally falling to her knees. Epic and heroic! Kerri Strug had the focus to help her override her pain. That is what creating a Compelling Vision will create for your client. Strug did, indeed, win the gold medal!

INSIST: Having a Compelling Vision creates a deep desire to succeed. Such was the case for a door-to-door fax machine sales rep whose vision was to start her own company. Perhaps you have heard of Sara Blakely.[2] If not, you are more than likely to have heard of Spanx, Blakey's vision.[3] Starting with $5,000 USD, she has created a company that has sales of over $400 million USD annually. She owns 100% of the company. She doesn't spend much money on formal advertising. Blakely was insistent in not only getting the product created, but also in ensuring that it was sold in stores like Neiman Marcus. Her unrelenting efforts to achieve her vision have resulted in her being endorsed by Oprah Winfrey. The Compelling Vision becomes the necessary catalyst to muster the courage to persist, insist, and refuse to be denied.

STRENGTHEN: For 27 years Nelson Mandela was imprisoned by the South African government during the apartheid era.[4,5] He spent a great deal of time in solitary confinement, and was subjected to hard labor. His crime was to ask for equality, an end to institutional racism, and for true democracy in South Africa. His three-hour speech during his trial ends with him saying, "It is an ideal for which I am prepared to die." When he was released, over a quarter of a century later, the government believed that he would be too old and feeble to create the change that he had fought for all of his life. They were wrong. His vision of a South Africa in which all citizens had equal rights and where every adult would have the right to vote for a government of their choice quickly came to fruition. He won the first ever free and fair elections in South Africa and became President. Mandela put an end to apartheid and helped heal a nation. His vision had kept his spirit alive and his imprisonment had only strengthened his beliefs.

HOPE: Hope is a future-oriented term—the feeling and expectation of a positive outcome. It is a fact that we will all, at some point or another, have difficult moments in our lives. Regardless of how affluent, confident, or prepared we believe that we are, challenging times will befall us all. It is at these moments, when we are thinking about how bleak our situation is, that we need a vision to help align our current actions with our future selves. One of my favorite movies, *The Shawshank Redemption*, illustrates how a Compelling Vision can help to shape and motivate a person even in dismal circumstances. Wrongly convicted for a crime he did not commit, Andy Dufresne (played by Tim Robbins) is sentenced to life in prison. Andy places a poster of Rita Hayworth on his jail cell wall. To Andy, the poster reminds him of the outside world, a place he has a vision of returning to. It also hides the tunnel he spends 25 years digging with a tiny rock hammer. Andy manages to escape and live as a free man, his vision realized. The whole film is built around the idea of hope—that Andy can and will live a better life in the future.

Your Past Is Your Guide—Not Your Definition

Farhan was born before Zimbabwe gained its independence in 1980 and grew up in the segregated Ridgeview neighborhood of the capital city, now named Harare. The colonial British regime drew lines to separate the minority Whites and the rest of the population. Ridgeview was one of the few neighborhoods reserved for people who were of Indian descent and regarded as second-class citizens. The Black Zimbabweans were considered to be third-class and mainly lived in high-density townships.

The White European citizens lived mostly in the suburbs to the north-east of the Central Business District (CBD). City planning had been strategically undertaken to benefit the colonialists. My father explained to me that when commuting into the city center for business, which was mostly done in the morning, the colonialists wanted to have the rising sun behind them. Likewise, when they were done with business, their drive home was comfortable as the sun was setting in the rear view mirror rather than blinding them.

Ridgeview residents faced the blinding sun both to and from the CBD.

Any non-White person in Zimbabwe was indoctrinated and made to believe that the Europeans were better, superior, and had the divine right to rule and discriminate against non-Whites. For Farhan and many others, the eventual liberation and independence of Zimbabwe didn't suddenly change that view, even when they attended desegregated schools.

After high school, Farhan had the opportunity to study abroad and attended the University of Nebraska-Lincoln (UNL), where he studied architecture. It was finally through his physical removal from Zimbabwe that he began to see himself as equal to anyone of any ethnic background. All of sudden, it was much closer to a level playing field. He was no longer a second-class citizen.

I talked with Farhan Khan, who is now the CEO and co-founder of Heritage Communities, headquartered in Omaha, Nebraska. This senior living development is characterized by very attractive masonry work, water features (ponds and fountains), and wonderful living spaces that boast expansive rooms filled with natural light. It is clear that his skill and passion for architecture has been applied towards achieving excellence in the design of the communities. In addition, the leadership model and philosophy of the company along with the exceptional "activities of daily life" programming for their residents completes a wonderfully executed mission.

Farhan's Indian-Zimbabwean background has also played a huge role in the culture of Heritage communities. "Respect for elders and hospitality is key," he stresses with passion.

In his mission statement as the CEO, Farhan vows that his company will hold itself to the highest standards and continuously strive to provide the best services and amenities: "One where every resident would be treated like part of my family."[7] The company has held true to that standard in all 13 communities they now run across Nebraska, Iowa, and Arizona.

This calm, softly spoken yet passionate leader told me that over the years his views have evolved as he and the business have grown. "I wanted to make sure that I did things the right way and be financially viable. Be comfortable." In the early days he was working 80 hours a week. Shortly after his father had passed away, the huge financial strain shaped how he approached his business: "I was committed to working hard for something that I could be proud of." Now Farhan has achieved his goal, he derives satisfaction from seeing the success of young people he saw potential in and hired. But the most fulfilling thing for him—the icing on the cake—comes when he sees those he has invested in go on to invest in others and make a positive impact on their lives.

Instead of mirroring the way that he was treated when growing up—denied freedom and having his ambitions suppressed—Farhan elevates those around him.

How to Create a Vision

One of the most effective methods for creating a vision is elucidated in Cameron Herold's book, *Double Double: How to Double Your Revenue and Profit in 3 Years or Less.*[8] Herold engineered the spectacular growth of 1-800-GOT-JUNK? from being a $2 million USD company to having a turnover of $106 million USD in just six years.[9] He writes about how the concept of creating a vision is an essential first step for a company that desires to be great if they want to experience fast growth.

This same notion applies to people that you coach. Their greatness begins by creating a Compelling Vision that, from the Dream Catcher perspective, will be synonymous with a vivid dream. As a coach, you should also take yourself through this process.

Below, I give examples of how some of my clients have been given prompts to get the process started.

There are many others available at **www.idreamidare.com**.

Examples of Compelling Vision Prompts

My Compelling Vision

DRE▲M
CATCHER

1. I'm happiest when...

2. Imagine that you traveled in a time machine into the future. The date is
   ____. Three years from now. You are in your workplace; walking and
   writing on a notepad.

   - What do you see?
   - What do you hear?
   - What are other staff saying?
   - What's the buzz?
   - Imagine a reporter is brought in to observe and write about you. After
     spending two weeks with you, what do they write about you?
   - What comments about work do you and your closest teammates make at
     happy hour?
   - What do others say about your leadership style?
   - How is your team running day to day? (e.g. Is it organized, exposed, keeping
     trains running on time etc. ?). What unique opportunities do you have?
   - What kind of stuff do you do every day? (Is your focus on strategy, team
     building, etc.)
   - How are core values being realized among you and your team?
   - What does work–life harmony mean and look like to you?

   Include comments on your values and on employee engagement. Include the
   type of interactions you have with staff. Remember that you are envisioning all
   these aspects of your team(s) and how you relate to them.

3. These are the five words I want to be used to describe me?

Dream Dare Do!

Depending on who you are working with, determine the type of prompts they will best respond to. Cameron Herold, coming from a business coaching perspective, encourages introspection when answering the following questions: "What are clients saying about you?"; "What kind of comments are your employees making at the water cooler?"; and "How is the company running day to day?" For those with a bigger scope of influence and responsibility in the organization such as directors and C-Suite executives, you must cover every area of your business. This includes culture, staff, marketing, public relations, IT, operations, finance, engineering, production, customer service, and so on.

The scope to which your client is able to dream is usually an indicator of how curious they are and also how much access they have to different areas of the organization. If their dream is limited because of a lack of access, you should help expand their limited understanding of the organization. If you determine that this limitation is because of their lack of curiosity, part of the plan for your client should include strategies for them to increase their drive to pursue learning.

When it comes to a compelling vision, it is important to think big about your life.

Notes

1. Kouzes, J. M., & Posner, B. Z. (1987). *The leadership challenge: How to get extraordinary things done in organizations.* San Francisco, CA: Jossey-Bass.
2. Sara Blakely Biography. (2016, March 14). Retrieved from https://www.biography.com/people/sara-blakely-031416
3. https://www.spanx.com/saras-world
4. https://www.bbc.com/news/world-africa-23618727
5. Mandela, N., & Quayson, A. (2002). *No easy walk to freedom.* London, England: Penguin.
6. https://www.heritage-communities.com/letter-from cco
7. Cameron Herold. (n.d.). Retrieved from https://www.cameronherold.com/
8. Herold, C. (2011). *Double double: How to double your revenue and profit in 3 years or less.* Austin, TX: Greenleaf Book Group Press.

9

Elements for a Compelling Vision

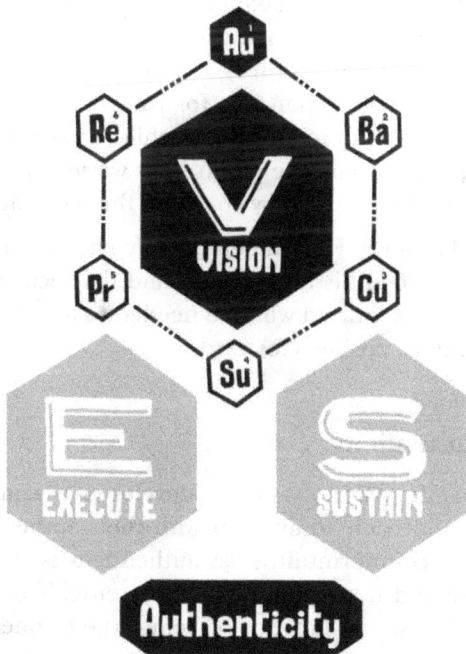

Dream Catcher, pages 101–117
Copyright © 2019 by Information Age Publishing
All rights of reproduction in any form reserved.

Seventy-five percent of startup businesses will fail.[1] That very scary statistic is something that Farhan Khan and I discussed when we met. He joked that entrepreneurs figuratively jump off a cliff in the hope that they will grow wings on the way down. Perhaps the reason for this is that, as an entrepreneur, it is important to have great confidence in your abilities—to believe that you can do it all. As with most entrepreneurs, Farhan had to multitask when he started out. He assumed the role of CEO but also had responsibility for marketing, sales, HR, payroll, maintenance, and so on. He acknowledges that he wasn't as skilled at everything as others could have been, but it was a matter of necessity. Perhaps one of the problems that lead to only a quarter of new businesses succeeding is because those in key roles literally lie to themselves that they are capable of doing it all. Imagine a heart surgeon who told himself that he was also a capable brain surgeon?

Farhan has come across people in business that fake competence. He stressed that in his business those that do this need to realize that this could lead to someone getting hurt. To succeed, you need to be authentic and honest about what you can do well and then work on your shortcomings.

The other aspect to the old maxim of being "true to oneself" relates to those with a victim mentality. Too many people externalize blame and place the responsibility for things that don't go well on everything and anyone but themselves. You should be responsible for your own actions. Even as parents it is important for us not to look at our children as perfect little beings. Farhan argued that we should see children as we see ourselves. Capitalize on their strengths and help them by coaching them on their weaknesses.

Given his background, Farhan could easily have externalized many of his problems and blamed his background and the societal issues he grew up with. Instead, he recognized what he needed to focus on internally and pushed himself and his business forward.

Bravery for Authenticity

It is imperative that the vision your client develops is as compelling as it can be and that they approach attaining it with their authentic and genuine self. This can seem counterintuitive, as authenticity is about facing up to who you really are and not living a life of pretense. This is, however, the perfect time to exercise the practice of being true to oneself. In fact, it is the safest time to truly reveal what lies within.

If the exercise of establishing a Compelling Vision was performed as an inquisition and asked, "Why haven't you accomplished the things you have always wished for in life?" it would be a disheartening—even devastating—process. But the Dream Catcher process confronts these challenging questions in a manner that creates the real possibility for an attainable future. It creates confidence—and the confident are brave!

Once you have the courage to ask the difficult questions you can start to dig into fundamentals such as:

- Am I living my life based on someone else's terms?
- Do I make myself a priority?
- What is the life I want to have and lead?
- Is my life based on design or mere circumstance?
- Am I being successful as a leader within my organization?

This enables you and your client to set concrete areas that need to be addressed, skills that need to be learned, and what support is needed to facilitate success.

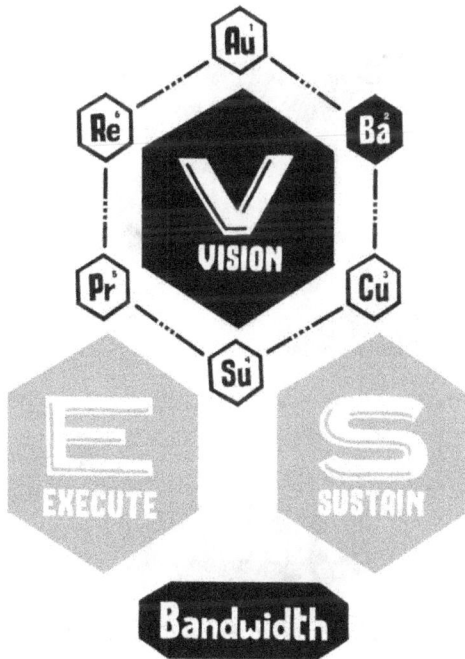

The Rise of a Change-Maker

Even before a plan to attain a Compelling Vision has been developed, many Dream Catcher clients have asked how they can take immediate steps towards the future they desire. Others have been overwhelmed and are not sure where to begin. However, all have exhibited a desire to change the course of their lives. The first step isn't about comparing and contrasting their current situation with a mental image of their future. Instead they need to free themselves from the factors limiting their ability to change.

The Dream Catcher process challenges self-doubt by asking clients how they can attain the skills they lack and close The Gaps they have acknowledged. This is the beginning of the "If I could" mindset.

The development of this belief and having a growth mindset makes the "Execution" phase of the Dream Catcher process much smoother and leads to building new habits that sustain both newly acquired skills and the ongoing learning process.

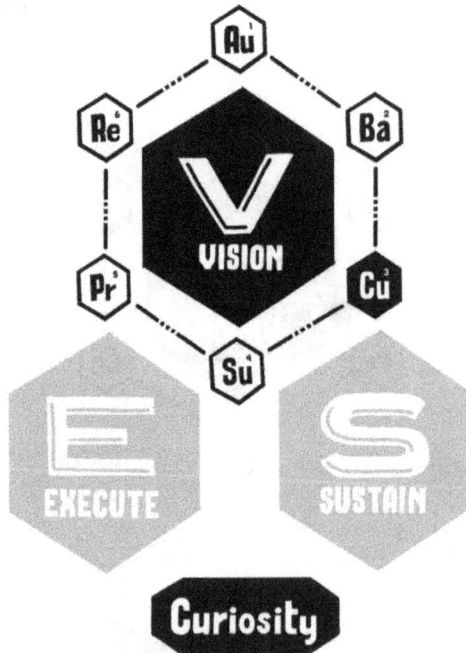

Curiosity

Curiosity has played a key role in Farhan's vision for the success of Heritage Communities. His big dreams meant that he had a clear mental image for the future of his company. Today, he attends global leadership conferences around the world and has an extensive network of resources that he can call on for support and advice. However, this isn't what he has learned the most from. He is curious—always looking for the "why" behind things. Farhan will observe, watch, and listen whenever he can. When he meets people, he listens. It doesn't matter if it's a CEO or a janitor—everyone has something they know. When he hears something that is profound or that he was previously unaware of, he makes a mental note of it. Later, he digs deeper into the thought, assessing whether or not it could add value to his business or life.

Awaken the Learner

With tremendous consistency, Dream Catcher clients who have gone through the process of developing a Compelling Vision have increased their sense of curiosity. Going through the process of painting a clear mental picture of their future started them on the path of wondering what else they hadn't thought through properly, what they do not know. They start asking questions and working towards acquiring and learning skills that will close The Gap between where they are today and where they desire to be in three years' time. It is amazing how looking further down the road creates questions about what lies ahead and how to reach out and seize it. The curious minds I have worked with have become acclimatized to this idea and happy getting outside of their comfort zones—to the place where their ideal future resides.

> "A DREAM IS NOT SOMETHING THAT YOU WAKE UP FROM. INSTEAD A DREAM IS SOMETHING THAT WAKES YOU UP."
>
> —Anonymous

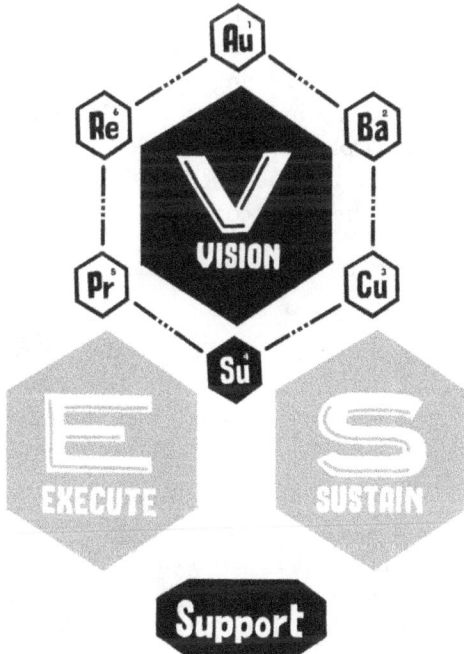

The morning that I met Farhan I was welcomed at the reception area by a well-mannered young woman. She couldn't have been much older than 13 years old! She was busy around the office answering and transferring calls, brewing coffee, and making photocopies. I later learned that this was his daughter. This was an idea that Farhan had been encouraged to try by a friend at Entrepreneur's Organization (EO).[2] Farhan had complained about not spending enough time with his daughter and his friend suggested that he bring her into the office to help out over the summer.

Farhan told me, "Most of my friends are business owners." He has surrounded himself with people like him—thriving, successful business people. This isn't just because he happens to move in these circles. It is a deliberate step that has helped him be the best he can be in business and in life. In 2003, he joined EO, which he said has helped to challenge and improve him. His company has grown from 30 employees in Omaha to now over 1,000 team members around the country.

Farhan explained how the people in this network have a keen interest in helping each other's businesses, but, more importantly, helping each other when it comes to life in general. It's personal first and business second. He knows and cares about the families, spouses, kids, and personal health of his EO friends.

He is also proud of the people that he has introduced into his business. For example, as a visionary, he knows that his rapid-fire creativity can be overwhelming to some. Heritage Communities Vice President Amy Birkel is a key person that he values for being an "integrator"—someone able to assess the many ideas that he has, slow things down, and create a fit for them in the organization's plans. "Maybe it doesn't fit in the one-year plan, however, it may fit in down the line. She helps lay things out so they don't disrupt the operations of the whole company."

The Network Developer

Despite some of my clients being quiet, private, and reserved, they have made some significant changes in their lives after creating their Compelling Vision. With their ideal self in mind, they have been challenged to look around them and ask the question, "Am I surrounded by people who improve or diminish me?"

They may not have started out with the right people around them or with the skillset to assemble a personal board of advisors (PBA), but once Dream Catcher's methods were applied they changed things and developed a network of individuals that could be utilized for their development.

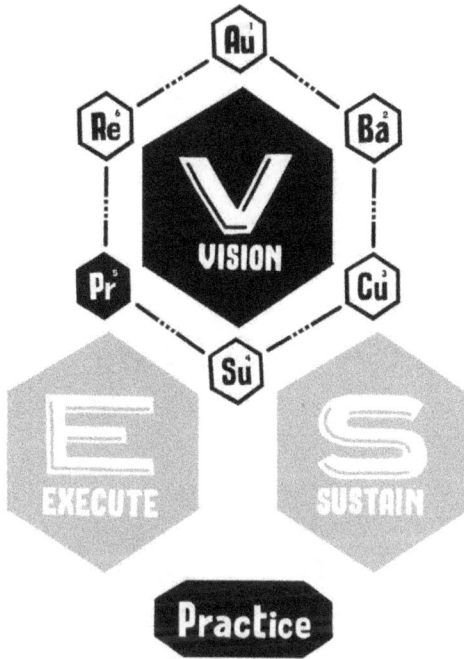

The Element of practice has an important role in creating a Compelling Vision. This is where your client begins to lay the foundation for routines that will enable them to execute, via actionable steps, and sustain their new habits. Practice, in relation to developing a Compelling Vision, is centered on learning how to dream big. This can be a challenge because of a lack of confidence, cultural issues, upbringing, and many other factors. Limiting one's ability to dream big is a habitual behavior that must be unlearned. Learning to dream big often takes practice.

The Commitment to Discipline

If a client doesn't manage to create a Compelling Vision, you must analyze why this may be. When the reasons provided by the client externalize blame, it is a red flag. You must reexamine the process that your client used. How much time did they spend on the exercise? The work put into creating the Compelling Vision is a good predictor of how things will go in the execution phase. At this juncture, a coach must examine their client's routines and habits. And they must assess whether those routines and habits support the client's commitment to discipline. To ever begin developing new skills, the client must understand that practice is critical.

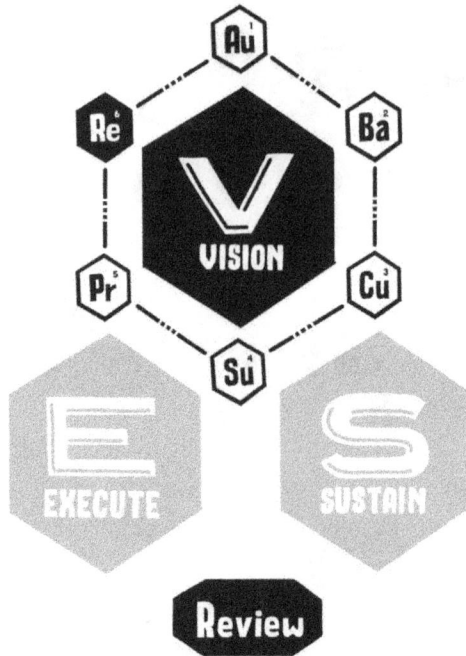

The principles of Review require your client to reflect on progress towards achieving their Compelling Vision. At times this may mean that you, as the coach, will critique past performance. However, this is really about being reflective through an introspective process. The coach should utilize the compelling vision in sessions and encourage the client to develop the ability to independently reflect on progress towards realizing it.

Create the Visionary

Some people don't consider themselves as visionaries, but ultimately, your client will develop the ability to dream. The vision creation process helps to develop creative individuals who can produce insightful and intriguing Compelling Visions that translate into all aspects of their lives.

How successful their attempts are to attain this vision will depend on how far the coach can get them out of their comfort zone. The more they hold onto the status quo the less likely it is that the vision will come to fruition. The beginning of this coaching journey for your client depends upon them being capable of imagining a compelling future life—one that clearly defines what success means to them personally. Here is the process your client should use to create their Compelling Vision:

1. FIND YOUR BEACH: Identify the place you love the best. A place where you can clear your mind and dive deep into your thoughts. Make it relaxing and intellectually engaging. For some it could be sitting in their favorite room at home, or sitting on the beach on a warm day. This place should never be the office or other common work areas.

2. ELIMINATE DISTRACTIONS: Get rid of your computer, phone, and any other devices that are distractions. Only reintroduce them into your environment when you are ready to be distracted. This is a time to be intensely focused.

3. TAKE A GOOD LOOK INTO THE FUTURE: Look at where you would like to be in three years' time. How do you get there? What changes do you need to make? What new skills do you need to learn?

4. WRITE IT DOWN: Use a pen and paper to map out what you see as the epitome of personal success. Describe it in detail. Imagine you are a journalist writing about every aspect of your life. How are you doing at work, in your life and your relationships? What do you do after work for enjoyment? What are your major accomplishments?

5. DREAM BIG AND DON'T HOLD BACK: The bigger and more ambitious your dream is, the better. Don't dream to scale or limit the possibilities by being overly realistic. Write down a wish list of what you really want.

After your client has spent time on this task, they must return to you with a clear picture of who and where they want to be in three years' time.

The Vision: Developing a Plan

When your client has successfully mapped out their Compelling Vision, the next stage is to review it with them. It is important that the coach has the right approach before entering into this meeting. Start with the end in mind. You must first want to understand your client's Compelling Vision so that you both have a clear idea of what the final picture looks like. This will also help you get an understanding of your client's values and desires. This knowledge is the foundation for developing the right plan and having your client commit to work on it and take the right steps to achieve the skills they need to attain success.

Start by asking them how the process of creating the vision was for them. Where and when did they do this and how much time did it take to complete? These details will give you an understanding of the process that your client used, which may also give you some idea of how they will apply themselves going forward into the execution phase of the program.

Everything your client writes down is vital for you to hear. There may be some repetition but even when your client wants to skip over certain aspects, insist that you want to hear everything. Use the techniques that we have covered in thinking, talking, and acting like a coach. You will have to work hard, but it's essential that you ensure your client leaves the meeting feeling empowered and inspired.

Of course, this is not about you and all about your client. The meeting should be held in a safe environment where they are at ease and comfortable with openly sharing their thoughts. There should be ample time set aside and you should have no distractions. The meeting should evidently not be in a public place, as clients can get emotional when sharing their innermost feelings. You should be prepared to help your client expand on particular points. Listen intently. If what your client has written down as part of their Compelling Vision means much more than they believe, politely ask for clarification. The following is an example of how to make sure that this process goes well.

Ask Questions:

Remember how important it is that coaches create a rich dialogue to enable effective communication. Do not ask questions in a manner that introduces fear, agitation, or mistrust into your relationship with your client. Ask politely, compassionately, and with keen interest. For example:

- Can you tell me more about...?
- Please help me understand what you mean by that?
- How are you feeling about...?
- I think I am following what you are saying, but please, could you rephrase the last part?
- Can you elaborate further on what you mean by that?

Getting to the Heart of the Compelling Vision

- Take a close look at the Compelling Vision and have your client elaborate on what each part of it means. What they have written down isn't enough. Additional depth to their aspirations will be revealed by carefully drilling down to what lies beneath.
- Take note of any repetitive points. This is a sign of recycled thoughts, also known as "looping." It is also worth noting whether or not the repetition reflects specific priority areas. This will be

covered in the next chapter when we discuss creating a plan to achieve the vision.

- There will likely be big umbrella points such as "organize my life." Listen attentively and help distill the client's thoughts in such areas to get into the specifics.

This is where you get to ask more questions and apply your abilities as a coach to listen extremely carefully.

You will do two things:

1. Probe so that you get more detail about the journaling the client has done to arrive at the Compelling Vision. Push them to think deeper.

   For example:

   Elaborate a little bit more about...

   What do you mean when you say...?

   Why is that of importance to you?

2. Clarify that what you think you are hearing is correct. Make sure you understand the vision in the same way as your client. You must be able to see it through their eyes.

   For example:

   Did I hear you say...?

   Did I understand you correctly when you said...?

   Is it accurate to summarize what you just said by stating...?

Mirroring is another key tool to encourage your client to elaborate further. In fact, it is probably one of the most underused yet most effective communication and persuasion techniques. FBI negotiator Chris Voss wrote about this technique in his book on negotiation skills.[3] Instead of asking a direct question or probing for further elaboration, repeat the last one to three words your client said back to them. This is one of the quickest ways to establish a rapport with your client and allow them to feel safe enough to fully reveal their inner truths. When done with an inflection and a pause, mirroring sounds like a question, and your client will offer further details without actually being directly asked, "What do you mean by that?"

This process will help you get a clear picture on whether your client is dreaming big enough. If not, it's an opportunity to help them dream bigger. As you understand more about what your client's Compelling Vision is and why it's so important to them, the next important step is to understand where they are right now in relation to their vision. This is "The Gap."

The Gap

The Gap is the space between where your client is today and where they want to be. This is vital to identify, as your help will be essential in closing it. You need to assess the tools that your client already possesses to close The Gap and what additional resources and support may be needed.

Explain The Gap

Once again, as a coach, it is time for you to listen. Why does The Gap exist? Why has your client, so far in their life, not been able to achieve their dreams? Knowing the answers to these questions will help unlock truths that assist both of you.

Having guided your client to this point you must now discover what the hurdles are to achieving their dream. If your client has a novel Compelling Vision, it may be useful to look back on their previous experiences and reflect why they have not been able to attain their aspirations earlier in life. If, however, your client has previously attempted to close evident gaps to attain their vision you will have to examine the process that they used and why it did not succeed.

The goal is to get a good idea of how your client works and what they have already tried. This understanding improves collaboration and reduces a client's resistance. You'll see the benefit of this collaboration in the event that you must replicate an already tried-and-failed method, perhaps one the client had previously misapplied or attempted at the wrong time of life. This collaboration also helps you know what to avoid. Sometimes traumatic experiences act as a block against certain techniques or methods. If, in attempting to close a gap, your client was deeply affected by failing, then the same approach is unlikely to work a second time around.

Start Actionable Items to Close The Gap

The Compelling Vision has led you and your client to delve deeper into why there's a gap between where they are and where they are trying to go. It is now time to plan with your client how The Gap should be closed. The following steps will help you create a plan with your client that will help them realize their compelling vision.

Recycled Thoughts: A Starting Point

Bitterness, anger, tension, angst, conflict, and inner turmoil are just a few of the negative thoughts that human beings can have. Since 2003, The National Science Foundation (NSF) has issued several reports regarding the number of thoughts the average human produces each day—between 15,000 and 70,000.[4,5] These are evidently very significant numbers!

It was also estimated that, on average, although our brain produces up to 70,000 separate thoughts every day, 95% of these thoughts are repeated daily.[6] With only 5% of what our brain produces being novel or unique to a particular day, it is clear that our core attitudes, mindsets, and beliefs are largely comprised of the consistent 95% of thoughts that the brain generates.

Understanding recycled thoughts is very important for you as a coach. As you review everything that your client wrote down or further explained during the process of creating their Compelling Vision, you should look and listen keenly for repetitive areas. They will certainly exist if your client followed the process correctly, and you should be able to identify them if you facilitated the subsequent meeting as prescribed by using the questioning methods we discussed earlier.

Identifying recycled thoughts is the Dream Catcher coach's window into understanding their client more deeply. When you dig deeper into these and work to deconstruct them, both you and your client will understand their significance. They are golden nuggets that will play a huge role as you begin to plan for your client's gap closure and skill acquisition process.

Considerations Before Finalizing the Plan

It is time to look ahead and envisage where you're taking your client. Look at the Elements tool kit and decide which ones are needed the most at this time. What skills, abilities, and resources does your client already possess in relation to their vision? What do they need? If they have been stuck in a rut, it's likely because of one and sometimes a combination of the following two reasons.

1. They have had the tools all along, but simply haven't been using them (they either didn't know they had them, didn't know how to use them, or didn't want to use them).
2. Their tool kit is under-equipped. The tools they have in hand are insufficient to realize their vision.

Thus, to help your client, you must establish why they haven't already helped themselves. Not only is this a matter of identifying The Gap, your client must explain why The Gap exists. This means that they must elaborate, clearly, why they have not already realized what they are striving for. You must approach this process as a way of building trust and not simply exposing vulnerabilities. This will help them analyze and recognize what tools they have and what they will need to equip themselves with going forward—including tools that they may be uncomfortable with utilizing. This process of analysis is not about dwelling in a maudlin way on the past, or placing blame, it is about helping them to understand the hurdles they may have faced and how, when they come up again (and they will), they can clear them.

If you have followed the process so far, you and your client will have laid the foundation for success. But be aware, there are no shortcuts. It will take hard work from both of you.

You will continue to develop the plan in the next chapter before your client puts it into practice and begins to execute it. The next section provides more specifics on creating and working through the plan.

Plan, Then Execute

1. TRUST YOURSELF: Hold a session with your client to demystify the process through which they told their story. Let them know that they are among the very few who are brave enough to do this. Help them identify the fears they may have had prior to sharing their vision for the first time and how they now feel after sharing it. By doing so you will help them to trust in themselves. They will recognize that they have faced and overcome the fears that everyone must contend with. The takeaway: Trust yourself and it will be easier to trust others.
2. FEAR SETTING: "Be Prepared!" Help your client anticipate problems and not blindly walk into situations that they have fears about. When they identify a fear, ask them the question: "What if that fear

became a reality, what would you do then?" An important resource that you should utilize and familiarize yourself with during this process is Tim Ferriss' exercise that he calls "fear-setting."[7] Ferriss presents this idea as a tool for people who tend to overthink ideas to the extent that they become paralyzed when making challenging decisions. It is a pretty good method that helps people quickly work through the consequences of taking or not taking an action. It has proven to be effective for some clients I have worked with as they worked to overcome the fear of making difficult choices. The aim is to psychologically prepare your client for some of their fears being realized. Would this kill them? Unlikely. Help them look ahead, anticipate, envision, and visualize positive thoughts.

3. IDENTIFY THE CHALLENGES: Your client has likely always known what they needed to confront in order to get to where they want to be, but they have typically avoided doing this. Challenge them to try and identify and confront the issues that they find difficult. One example relates to a person that I was coaching who had very low self-esteem, despite being in a leadership position. They feared asking for help because of not wanting to admit weakness. After acknowledging their lack of confidence and finally confronting it through this process, a focus of our work centered on improving their self-esteem. My client could no longer struggle as the leader of a team as this was limiting how effectively it could fulfill its mission. This was not the biggest challenge my client faced, but it was one that manifested itself in everyday life and affected other relationships. Our process led to a successful outcome and my client is now a fearless VP in their company. In order to really help your client you must encourage them to step outside of their comfort zone and deal with what they find as difficult and sometimes frightening situations.

4. LEARN FROM LESSONS OF FAILURE: There will be tough lessons to be learned in the journey that you take with your client. Sometimes clients will stumble and not achieve the outcomes that they want. They must have resilience and a positive mindset before taking the first steps. For example, you could agree a statement such as: "If I don't achieve the expected outcome this time, I will try differently by. . . ." Without having this mindset, there are very high chances that a major setback will cause them to quit the program. They may also externalize and look to place the blame elsewhere instead of considering what they could have done differently and applying that to their next attempt.

5. BE TRANSPARENT: You must be clear that this process is not going to be easy. But if your client believes in you and trusts the program they are also going to learn to believe in themselves. They will grow

in confidence. Every time they fall, your client will bounce back as a stronger and wiser person. Moreover, they will never have to fake it, for they will learn how to truly make it.

COMPELLING VISION SUMMARY	
Goal	• Understand their Compelling Vision • Hear their voice • Understand their values • Empower • Inspire
Prepare	• The right environment for your client (venue, setting) • Have an open mind • Be ready for tears • Distraction free • Look for recycled thoughts
Tone	• Smiling • Encouraging • Reassuring • Interested
Questions	• Dream Catcher queries (e.g., "tell me more about that") • Effective pauses • Mirroring (instead of a question, repeat the last three or four words your client says with a question-like inflection) • Highlight recycled thoughts (You mentioned that three times earlier. It must be important)
Plan	• Determine the Compelling Vision • Explain The Gap • Develop a plan to close The Gap • Execute

SUMMARY

Vision:

- ▪ The vivid mental picture of an ideal future.
- ▪ The beginning of a journey and a blueprint for life.
- ▪ Helps with FISH which is important for the coaching process.

Application of the Elements to create a Compelling Vision:

- ▪ Be true and comfortable with yourself (Authenticity).
- ▪ Assess what you know and compare that with what you would like to know and how much you can give in terms of time and emotions (Bandwidth).
- ▪ Awaken the learner (Curiosity).

- Surround yourself with those who can help you dream (Support).
- Be disciplined. Exercise the art of journaling (Practice).
- Be reflective about the introspective processes. Evaluate the Compelling Vision with the coach (Review).

Developing a plan with a client after a Compelling Vision is created:

- Get a deep understanding of your client's vision. Use rich dialogue as you review it.
- Ask and listen. Find the "sweet spot of dialogue."
- Look for patterns. Understand recycled thoughts and themes.
- Drill down on generalizations to get to what lies beneath.
- Understand what The Gap is and ask your client to explain their understanding of it.
- Devise a plan to close The Gap.

You are now ready to begin to work on the "12-Week Focus Areas," the Execution phase of VES.

Notes

1. Gage, D. (2012, September 20). *The venture capital secret: 3 out of 4 start-ups fail.* Retrieved September 09, 2018 from https://www.wsj.com/articles/SB1000087 2396390443720204578004980476429190
2. Entrepreneurs' Organization (EO) is the world's only peer-to-peer network exclusively for entrepreneurs. See https://www.eonetwork.org/
3. Voss, C. (2017). *Never split the difference: Negotiating as if your life depended on it.* New York, NY: HarperBusiness.
4. http://www.loni.ucla.edu/About_Loni/education/brain_trivia.shtml
5. http://bit.do/edFu
6. Faith, Hope, & Psychology. (2012, March 2). *80% of thoughts are negative... 95% are repetitive.* Retrieved from https://faithhopeandpsychology.wordpress.com/2012/03/02/80-of-thoughts-are-negative-95-are-repetitive/
7. Ferriss, T. (n.d.). *Why you should define your fears instead of your goals* [TED talk]. Retrieved from https://www.ted.com/talks/tim_ferriss_why_you_should_define _your_fears_instead_of_your_goals

10

Execute

Doing It! The Challenge Begins!

I grew up in Mt. Pleasant, a suburb of Harare, the capital city of Zimbabwe. I am the fourth of six children and we all had chores to do. Despite having a gardener, I often found myself tending to our enormous vegetable garden, especially during school holidays. This consisted of pulling up weeds and watering the

> "DO OR DO NOT, THERE IS NO TRY."
>
> —Master Yoda

Dream Catcher, pages 119–127
Copyright © 2019 by Information Age Publishing

garden using a hose. I did my job diligently (or as meticulously as a 10-year-old can). But one day I decided that playing soccer and riding my bike was more important than doing a thorough job. That day my 45-minute routine to water the garden took me just 15 minutes. I gave it a light sprinkling and took off with my friends. That evening, like every other, my father asked me if I had done my chores and I responded affirmatively. It was the end of the conversation. Or so I thought. At about midnight my father woke me up. He told me that I needed to get dressed and head out into the garden with him. There was no purpose in asking questions about why we were heading into the dark of night. I figured out the reason rather quickly. My father didn't ask me many questions, which I now see was most likely by design. I would likely have been in deeper trouble by not responding truthfully in an attempt at self-preservation. My father had clearly seen that the garden was very dry and hadn't been properly watered. I didn't contest his findings, but I apologized and told him I would fix it. My plan was to do so in the morning as soon as I woke up. My father didn't share my sentiment. He wanted it done immediately. Suddenly, I was no longer sleepy. I knew that there could be no compromise. I told my father that I would connect the hose and get it done. He disagreed. "You had a chance to use the hose earlier," he said. Instead, he handed me a bucket and, along with his flashlight, headed back to the house, which suddenly looked quite far away. I was left to complete the job with no light apart from the moon.

My 45-minute job to thoroughly water the garden took over two hours. I had never been up that late working outside. Perhaps it was the overly cautious 10-year-old who was afraid. However, I recall hearing rustling of whatever night creatures were out moving around the yard—those sounds kept my attention and head on a swivel. Whatever it was, those strange sounds are as vivid today as they were that night.

Whether as a coach or a client, when we have the tools at our disposal, a major question must be answered. Are you being diligent and will you whole-heartedly accept the burden of any challenge upfront? Failure to do so, will not only leave you with the consequences of a job poorly done, but the responsibility to fix those consequences by way of a much more tedious and exhausting path.

Everyone comes into this world with talent. No matter what one's circumstances, we all have an ability—something that we can excel at. The difference between realizing that talent and achieving success or remaining stuck in the status quo is that not everyone has an equal amount of opportunity. For many, an opportunity, no matter how fleeting, will present itself in life, and must be seized. Some people create their own life chances; others need to learn to recognize and take those opportunities when they arrive. As people, we are in more control than we realize. Dream Catcher provides that window of opportunity. It is a chance to realize your talent, develop, and grow.

So far in this book we have discussed the method for creating a Compelling Vision and planning how your client can attain that vision. This is not enough. There are actions that must be taken! The plan must be executed.

When it came to watering the garden, I had all the tools and opportunities to accomplish my task effectively. I did not use them and I paid the price. You, of course, aren't a 10-year-old who skipped some chores.

Instead, you're a person who is making decisions that are hopefully based on your values, beliefs, and convictions. The ramifications for not following through on what you have promised yourself will profoundly affect you. It is now up to you to make the right decisions to reach your destiny.

For those who have the tools to enact the changes that are needed and either consciously choose to ignore them, deny that they exist, or believe that they aren't really available for people like them, life will be an uphill struggle.

Dream Catcher provides you with the tools and, along with your capacity to learn and apply, *you* create the opportunity. It doesn't matter how old, poor, or uneducated you are. It has no bearing on your social status in life. If you want to succeed, you must create the opportunity and then seize it.

It is time to look beyond dreaming. It is time to focus on taking action.

Dream Catcher realizes that people fundamentally know *what* they must do, but they struggle with *how* to do it. What follows is the Dream Catcher guide to Execution. Help your client use the Elements that we have discussed to attain their dreams by focusing on some key aspects of the journey.

The problem with execution isn't the desire of your client or a lack of ideas on how to move forward, rather it's being driven enough to do what it is we desire to do. There are many reasons that people cite when rationalizing why they don't do something that they know is beneficial and important to them. Reasons like:

- I don't have time.
- I won't be good at it.
- It's too difficult.
- How about next time?

These are simply excuses!

To overcome excuses and achieve what one desires to get out of life, it is essential to understand why great and compelling dreams fail. It is both complex and yet so very simple at the same time: You're doing the WRONG things to get what you want. This may not be because you lack a great plan to get ahead, but rather that some people tend to get stuck in the strategy phase. As the Chinese proverb states: "A journey of a thousand miles begins with one footstep."

The vast majority of professionals today can't identify what they *really* want to create and achieve in their lives. Dream Catcher has helped break through that barrier by focusing on the creation of a Compelling Vision. Still, many others who are able to dream and create their vision remain stuck with dreams that remain fleeting illusions.

Dream Catcher clients defy stasis, developing the capabilities they need to reach they future they desire. The following section outlines a continual process to ensure your client's success in achieving their Compelling Vision.

Learning Leaders

Remember my client Dr. C., the dentist? (Part I, pp. 9) He shared how it was less challenging for him to learn his medical competencies than to understand how to become an effective leader. That seems to be a sentiment echoed by other technically skilled professionals I have spoken with. Several academic papers have been written about this issue. One such article was presented to the Project Management Institute in 2010.[1] It concludes that it is easier to increase expertise in hard skills such as language proficiency, typing speed, machine operation, and computer programing, than soft skills. This is most likely because hard skills are easier to measure in terms of performance and many resources have been committed to increasing proficiency and expertise in them. Dream Catcher was designed to address the need for soft skill development. The program is able to effectively impact and improve the more difficult-to-learn soft skills such as communication, leadership, creativity, negotiation, decision-making, and conflict resolution. These are crucial skills for modern professional life and are often overlooked.

Dream, Dare, Do!

In September of 2016, I coached a new supervisor at QLI. She was knowledgeable of many managerial tasks, policy procedures, and the organization. When she created her Compelling Vision, a few of the professional things she wanted to attain revolved around wanting to be a leader that could develop other leaders. During one of our meetings, she helped me comprehend gaps that existed and why they were important for her to close. We looked at three areas that she was going to focus on. These were the most imperative and immediate areas that would ensure an effective start in closing The Gap. The areas we identified were:

The Art of Delegation

As she was transitioning to being a supervisor, one of the things that she was struggling with was empowering others. She had been an ideal team member prior to her promotion. Most things that needed to be handled, she tackled with more thoroughness than her teammates—including her supervisor. She had been very good at making sure that every detail was covered and would take the lead on handling any important matters that came up. She was also full of drive and compassion; she didn't want to burden her teammates with extra work and so led from the front, as the culture in the company preached.

In her transition to being a leader, this willingness to take responsibility for everything was causing problems. She not only had new duties such as helping the team develop in line with the organizational mission, she also had new routines, habits, and attitudes that needed to be adopted. Delegating would not only empower others in her team, but also free her to focus on the big picture.

Relationship Building

It is challenging to transition from being part of a team to being the supervisor of the same group of people. The relationship with newer team members that she worked with seemed strained. While still the team player everyone trusted, she felt removed from the colleagues she viewed as friends. As a leader, this affected how effective she was when it came to helping her team, including teaching them and challenging them to grow. There was work to be done on how she managed her relationships in this new role.

W.A.I.T. (Why Am I Talking?)

Together, we also looked into her tendency to dominate conversations and not effectively listen to others. She had come to the conclusion that she had to focus on the skill of active listening. We aimed for her to ask more questions and seek to understand her team members better so that she could be more effective in supporting them. This was something that was difficult for her to do in the heat of the moment, but she trusted the fact that becoming a better listener would help her immensely.

Within three months of the plan getting under way, her team members were writing notes to the CEO to express what an amazing team leader she was. One of her team members was nominated to become a mentor for others in the company—a practice that has led to QLI having unrivaled retention numbers when compared to the industry average. In the next year, two more of her team members were promoted and moved to other departments. Since then, she has become the leader that newer supervisors are paired with to learn from. She is a wonderful mentor to many and a major resource for myself. Many in the company seek her out for help with personal and personnel issues.

The Elements were applied to design her program for Execution and she had the necessary tools to support her. Her soft skills improved tremendously. She now works *on* the team, not *in* it.

Do the Necessary Things Critical for the Success of Your Vision

Narrow the Focus

One of the biggest struggles with execution is maintaining focus. Many people today boast about their ability to multitask, but neuroscience has debunked the theory that the human brain can effectively do this at all. It is a myth! People are not more productive through superior multitasking. In fact, the reverse is true. We are actually more distracted and less able to focus on specific tasks because all of our competing devices and tasks rob us of the ability to effectively focus, learn, and master what is important. It is simpler to juggle three balls than it is to juggle four, five, or six at the same time. When your attention is being demanded by competing elements in your life, it is even more challenging to learn. With this in mind, the Dream Catcher process instructs the coach to ideally focus on one key area at a time with a client and certainly not more than three.

Clear and Distinct Areas with Clear and Direct Methods

> "YOU DON'T GET RESULTS BY FOCUSING ON RESULTS. YOU GET RESULTS BY FOCUSING ON THE ACTIONS THAT PRODUCE RESULTS."
>
> -Mike Hawkins

So, as a coach, I will select up to three areas to focus on with my client, right? Wrong!

Remember the "Sweet spot of dialogue"? If you have exercised it effectively when getting your client to share their Compelling Vision, you will already have revealed what key area or areas your client should work on.

Many conceptualize coaching in terms of sports and competitive situations.[2] Research has shown that the quality of a sporting experience and the likelihood of an individual being motivated and staying in the sport is often determined by the climate created by the coach. This relies on satisfying three key psychological needs: autonomy, competence, and relatedness.

- Autonomy is feeling that you have control over your own actions.
- Competence is having a perception that you possess adequate ability.
- Relatedness is having a sense that you belong (to the group, coaching process, or sport).

How the coach should operate depends on the age of the group. The study cited separated participants into two main groups, 11- to 13-year-olds (youth) and 15- to 18-year-olds (adolescents).

The results revealed that athletes remained motivated and stayed with a sport when the coaches were mindful of certain things. With those in the youth age group, autonomy was seen as merely unwanted pressure. This group was more than happy to trust the coach to make decisions and explain why they were doing certain things and saw autonomy simply as the freedom to be able to voice whether or not they were enjoying the session.

When it came to adolescents, participants saw more value in being able to take ownership of their training routines despite understanding that it was the coach who provided the overall framework for the session. There were varying levels of maturation in the athletes studied, thus the timing of when they were given, or wanted, more ownership varied, but this was emphasized by the study as an important factor in keeping them involved. Finally, because these athletes had to balance educational demands with sport, the volume, intensity, and content of training needed to be negotiated with the coach.

Never approach coaching adults with the same methods one would use to coach 11- to 13-year-olds. Research shows that autonomy equals effectiveness and this is acknowledged in the Dream Catcher program. Together with your client you must identify a key area (and no more than three) where they will begin to focus on skill building. You are there to guide and not to dictate what this may be. Where you should take responsibility is in getting clarity on what specific methods your client plans on applying to develop skills in the focus area within the 12-week process.

Start Line, Finish Line, Deadline

As a coach you will now have helped your client to set the focus area (or areas) for the initial period of at least 12 weeks. You have a framework to set the plan so your client can take the specific steps to ensure that they learn skills that will move their Compelling Vision closer to reality. This creates common understanding that there is a time factor and with that comes a sense of urgency and accountability. What gets measured gets done! Setting timelines also helps your client prioritize and focus. There will always be urgencies in life, but your client should be able to delineate between what is urgent and what is important.

Some of my clients have had to develop their organizational and prioritization skills as a part of their coaching plan. This timeline tool was the biggest aid they had to close such gaps. They were able to apply this skill to other areas of their lives and saw positive results. It is important to remember that the timeline is not arbitrary, but should be fully agreed upon with your client who will then take on the responsibility of keeping to it. Your role is to challenge your client if they request a timeline that is either too long or short. During this period, you must be supportive but also candid about their performance.

The Element of authenticity will help the client take stock of their actions and be reflective. There should be no externalizing if they struggle to follow through. Dream Catcher processes have proven to be successful when clients believe that they are responsible if things do not go well. Of course, life can deliver catastrophes and calamities that are beyond anyone's control, but your client must limit excuses and maximize control of their own destiny.

The 12-Week Session

This is the minimum period that your client should focus on beginning to tackle their plan. It takes time to build a habit. The period of time spent on a focus area could be longer—that is something for you and your client to agree upon. But it is important to settle on a time frame that will really challenge your client, rather than allowing the process to meander. Start by telling your client that the deadline is 12 weeks. Having a clear finish line will ensure that your client is focused. Assure them that you will be available throughout this period and that the success of the program is not determined by the deadline, but rather by the quality and intensity of the effort they put into the process.

SUMMARY

Execute:

Your client will work on one focus area (and never more than three).

Your client will diligently apply themselves to the process and completing the necessary work.

Things to remember:

- Keep a narrow focus.
- Have clear and distinct goals and focus areas.
- Agree on the specific methods to be used.
- Accept no excuses from your client.

Advice for a coach to help engage and involve the client:

- Autonomy—The client has control over and responsibility for their plan.
- Competence—The client has confidence that they possess the adequate ability to execute.
- Relatedness—The client has a sense they belong and are worthy of coaching.

Set concrete dates:

- Start line: Begin with a minimum 12-week process.
- Deadline: The end date of the 12-week process agreed with your client.
- Finish line: The 3-year Compelling Vision.

Remember, what gets measured gets done!

Notes

1. De Piante, J. (2010). The soft part is the hard part. Paper presented at PMI® Global Congress 2010—North America, Washington, DC. Newtown Square, PA: Project Management Institute.
2. Alvarez, M. S., Balaguer, I., Castillo, I., & Duda, J. L. (2012). The coach-created motivational climate: Young athletes, well-being, and intentions to continue participation. *Journal of Clinical Sport Psychology, 6*(2), 166–179.

11

Elements to Execute

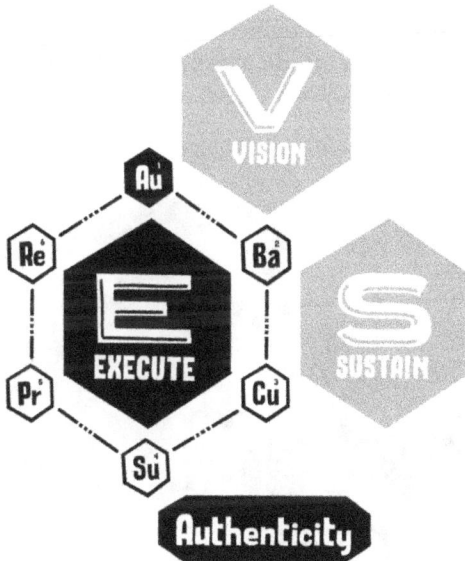

Practice is a critical Element necessary to help your client execute. Awareness is fundamental in order for your client to learn and develop the necessary skills. German philosopher Martin Heidegger is acknowledged to be one of the most original and important thinkers of the 20th century, and his most famous body of work is the unfinished *Being and Time*.[1] In it, Heidegger suggests that authenticity does not require remarkable effort or discipline, like meditation. Rather, it calls for a mere shift in attention and engagement—awareness. Dream Catcher attaches the same viewpoint to the Element of authenticity within the realm of execution. Your client must engage authentically with practice that enables learning for skill acquisition.

To reach a state of awareness, I encourage my clients to consistently apply time to practice the self-evaluation tools and methods that they have in their array of Elements.

- Disconnect from the computer and other devices.
- Use journaling.
- Try to keep a daily log of progress and successes.

By practicing such techniques, all of my clients have been able to self-assess themselves accurately. At times they have had to share their journaling with me to help me better understand what is going on. Great diagnosis leads to effective adjustment, if needed, to lead them to effective gap closure and skill acquisition.

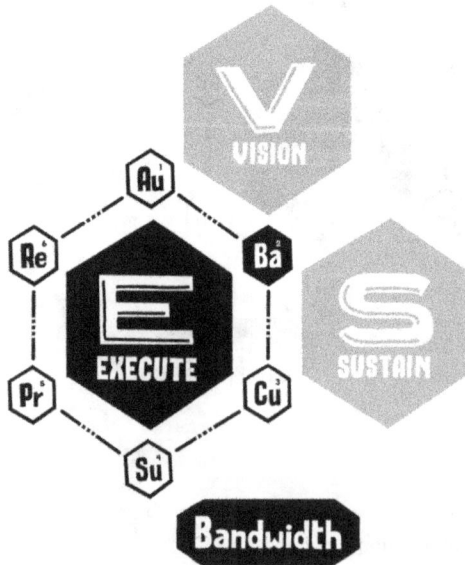

"The office team is struggling because she cares more about her own reputation and success than she does the team and the organization!"

Dan, a friend who also happens to be a member of a network of small business owners I work with, complained about the issues he was having with one of his recently promoted employees (who I will call Gabby). We discussed the issue at length from various angles, including the possibility that he may have made a mistake by promoting Gabby to her new position. Dan explained that there was nothing in her new role that she hadn't excelled at prior to the promotion. Gabby had worked hard during her first three years at the company and had been a standout, model employee. Her teammates respected her and she had mentored a number of them. She had been rewarded and recognized for her performance. But now that she had become a manager she was struggling. To Dan, it seemed as if Gabby had, all of a sudden, forgotten every trait and behavior that had earned her respect in the office.

I asked Dan how much responsibility Gabby had previously and how much she had now. It transpired that this was a lateral move in terms of responsibility, but a promotion on paper.

Dan's challenge was to understand something that I have seen many new leaders struggle with—especially people assigned to new roles in a familiar environment—still working with the same people and likely sitting at the same desk.

Within a week, Dan had determined that Gabby was definitely the right person for the job. She was back to her usual productive self and at the time of writing, Dan has disengaged from involvement in day-to-day operations and is focusing more on the development of his business.

What Dan was able to do in just a few days of observation was see how Gabby operated.

1. After promotion, Gabby still hung on to her previous roles despite the fact that Dan had shifted responsibilities to other team members. Gabby still handled her old caseload.
2. Whenever someone asked questions in the office, even when they were not directed to her, she would involve herself in providing the answer or finding a solution. Most of the time these were issues that other team members could handle without Gabby's involvement.
3. Gabby would take on additional commitments to deal with such issues. She would stretch herself and come in earlier and work later to do things that she didn't need to do. Her bandwidth for her new leadership role was compromised!

When Dan met with Gabby to discuss his observations, she was surprised to hear that she was doing these things. She admitted to Dan that she was feeling stressed and had been questioning whether or not it was time for her to move on. She was not being effective in handling her primary responsibilities. Dan asked her to hold off tendering her resignation and walked her through a few things he wanted her to do. As a result:

1. Gabby shifted to a different part of the office as a symbolic gesture to make clear that things were now different.
2. Gabby began to work on the team more than in it. She would plan at the beginning of the week what things she felt she needed to focus on to help the business continue to grow. She saw her colleagues as vital members in the process and her role as bringing out the best in them.
3. Gabby limited her involvement in problem solving trivial issues. Instead, she empowered the team members to discuss and solve such issues themselves. She made herself redundant from the role of being the minor problem solver.

With these simple steps, Gabby and the business began to operate as Dan hoped. He didn't lose one of his best leaders because she was taking on too much, being overwhelmed, and not having the time and space to do what she could do best.

He cleared up her bandwidth.

Mastery Over Mental Hijacks

In his book *Drive* Daniel Pink makes a compelling and thought-provoking case for motivation and what drives humans towards their goals.[2] In order to attain that intrinsic motivation, the book sets out the three parts of the motivation formula: autonomy, mastery, and purpose.

Your client wants to master the use of their newfound tools. Whether it's learning how to play an instrument, a new language, a skill at work, or how to have great inner dialogue, there is always an initial ecstatic feeling. At some point, this process can also be frustrating.

It isn't unusual if your client feels like they're not getting anywhere. That's a mental hijack! Pink drew from the work of psychologist Dr. Carol Dweck, who has been studying motivation and achievement in humans for decades.[3] It has been scientifically proven that as humans, our mindset determines whether or not we will succeed at what we do. Below are two types of mindsets that Dweck suggests will lead to either being hijacked or to realizing success.

In a *fixed mindset*, people believe their basic qualities, such as intelligence or talent, are simply fixed traits. They spend their time documenting their intelligence or talent instead of developing them. They also believe that talent alone creates success—without effort. They're wrong.

In a *growth mindset*, people believe that their most basic abilities can be developed through dedication and hard work—brains and talent are just the starting point. This view creates a love of learning and a resilience that is essential for great accomplishment. Virtually all successful people have these qualities.

The principles of Dream Catcher promote the notion that having a growth mindset is essential for mastery to be possible. You are prone to mental hijacks if you have a static and fixed mindset. You will not emancipate yourself.

If we believe that we can break free of our status quo through the growth mindset, we will liberate ourselves and advance to new heights.

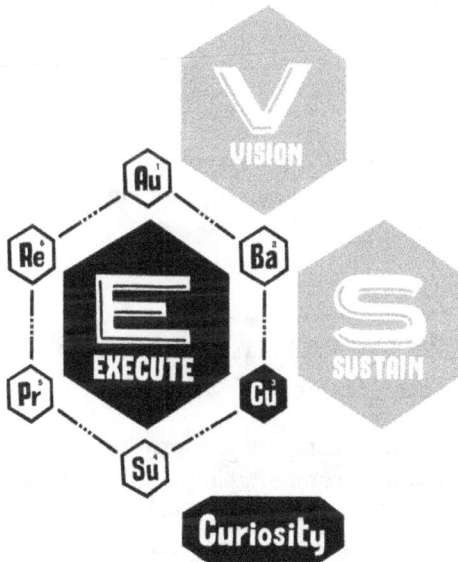

There are many variables that cause curiosity and enthusiasm to acquire new skills to die out for many people. We will explore some of the main reasons below.

Don't Make Them "Thunkers"

Children are naturally curious and have the desire to experiment and tinker. Unfortunately, this natural human instinct seems to be something that society appears to unconsciously see as deviant. Just look at how we teach and practice behavior that contradicts effective learning.

As a child, I remember hearing the famous proverb, "Curiosity killed the cat," which warns us against unnecessary investigation or experimentation. The less frequently heard rejoinder is "but satisfaction brought it back!"

One of my favorite examples of curiosity being suppressed is from a movie I watched in 2013 at the local theater with my wife and kids called *The Croods.*[4]

Despite the fact that this is essentially an entertaining family movie about cave people, a takeaway for me is a scene when the paternal character, Grug Crood, tells the story of "Krispy Bear" as a means to keep his family from leaving the safety of the cave. Krispy is a fictional bear made up by Grug to warn them of the dangers of the outside world.

Below is a short transcript of the movie scene.

> **Grug:** Tonight, we'll hear the story of Krispy Bear. A long time ago, this little bear was alive. She was alive, because she listened to her father, so she was happy. [Eep sighs] But Krispy had one terrible problem . . . she was filled with . . . curiosity! [Everyone gasps] Yes! And one day, she saw something new and died!
>
> **Thunk:** Just like that?
>
> **Grug:** Yes!
>
> **Gran:** Same ending as every day.
>
> **Thunk:** I get it, Dad. I will never do anything new or different.
>
> **Grug:** Good man, Thunk.

Maybe it's a stretch to compare modern humans to fictionalized animated cavemen. However, I contend that the themes from this DreamWorks movie aren't irrelevant when you analyze human behavior and how we choke and kill curiosity. Think back to how many times your own parents, when you asked the question "Why?" answered you with "Because I say so!"

Some of my clients have an insatiable appetite to learn. They are highly curious. Others fear to take the first step. Your client's growth and level of success will be catalyzed by their appetite for learning. If you have a client that appears to be apprehensive of learning, you can support them by finding out what most piques their interest.

How to Become Curious

1. Read an array of written material (blogs, books, articles, etc.) related to your interests—learn more about what you think you already know. Deepen your passions and immerse yourself in what you love.

2. Sharpen your mind using the minds of others: converse and consult with other people. It doesn't matter if they are like-minded thinkers or have different worldviews.

3. Don't be afraid of appearing to be unknowledgeable. I've seen people bite their lip because they are afraid of being seen as uninformed. Have courage and learn. Be willing to ask all sorts of questions, including what you think are the stupid ones.

4. Be a kid again. Always ask "Why?"

5. TEDx is a huge resource offering 15-minute videos on a vast number of topics, often related to personal or organizational development. These are jumpstarts to becoming curious to know more about many subjects.

6. Join a club or society that matches your interests, or join one to learn about something you want to know more about.

7. Learn a new thing such as a skill or a language. Start new hobbies.

8. Visit **www.idreamidare.com**. There are many resources for new learning there.

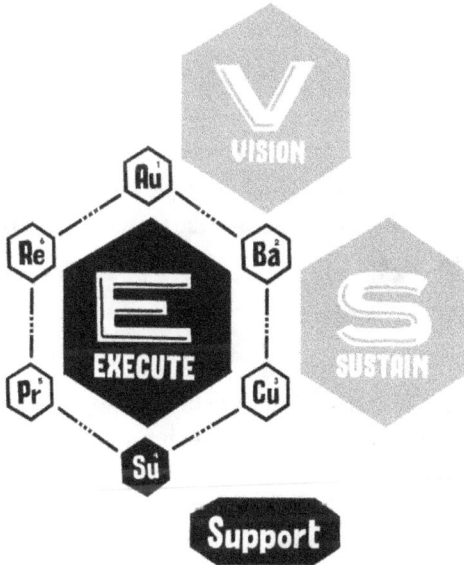

Share the Dream

Your client's personal board of advisors (PBA) is going to play a big role in their success in executing their plan. Encourage your client to share their Compelling Vision with their support network and get feedback on how to build the skills necessary to close their gap.

As your client shares their dream with others, several incredible things happen. Simply speaking the words and affirming that they are going to embark on a journey strengthens their sense of belief and determination to succeed. I once worked with a client who wanted to work on public speaking. They shared this aim with their PBA and a few others on their team. One person on the PBA asked if my client wanted to practice by helping facilitate a team meeting she had coming up. My client took the opportunity and used it as part of their development plan. There was also a skill building program that QLI had initiated in which team members were mentored on giving presentations. It focused on three areas: preparation, emotion, and technique (PET). My client was invited into the program and received a mentor. The progress made was impressive and my client eventually went on to represent the company as a very skilled conference presenter. Sharing the vision with a PBA creates a supportive group for your client who will not only provide other tools and opportunities, but also create a sense of accountability.

Accountability

What is measured gets managed. This dictum, simply put, means that regular measurement and reporting of performance keeps people focused.

Dream Catcher has a weekly review tool built into **www.idreamidare .com** that serves as an unambiguous method for measuring progress. This assists with accountability and is essential to the final piece of the VES process—"Sustain."

Huddle

In addition to the PBA, Dream Catcher clients also often meet up with each other to share progress, plans, success stories, and encouragement. This is an extra support network and allows clients to compare and contrast their experiences, deal with problems that they are facing, and draw inspiration from each other. I always remind my clients, "What you say and declare about yourself, you become."

To learn more about these support groups, visit **www.idreamidare.com**

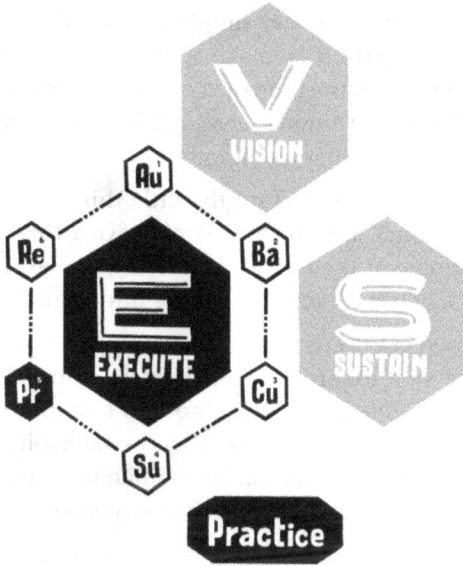

In the Execution stage of the Dream Catcher program, deliberate practice makes perfect. This is the key Element at this point of the program.

> "KNOWING IS NOT ENOUGH. WE MUST APPLY. WILLING IS NOT ENOUGH. WE MUST DO."
>
> —Johann Wolfgang von Goethe

Be Highly Structured

In order to facilitate that your client practices well you must:

- Determine and plan what skills your client will work on.
- Deconstruct each skill down to its most basic elements.
- Identify the most fundamental concepts and start with these.
- Establish routines and turn practice into a ritual by setting out the number of times a week, where, how, when, and with whom practice is undertaken.
- Establish the time frame—the start line to the deadline.
- Focus on one key area (and no more than three) at a time.
- Examine the Elements and determine which are most needed to ensure successful skill acquisition.

Make Your Bed

Admiral William H. McRaven, in his 2014 University of Texas Commencement speech, shared a very simple lesson.[5] If you want to change the world or yourself, start off by making your bed every morning. He explained that this not only sets a tone of accomplishment as the first order of the day, "but it will give you a small sense of pride and it will encourage you to do another task and another and another."

McRaven added, "If you can't do the little things right, you will never do the big things right." He concluded his advice by reminding us that when you return home at the end of a hard day, the last thing you do creates optimism for a better tomorrow. Getting into your already made bed!

Making your bed is a pretty straightforward means of developing a new habit. It is the first step towards the "Goldilocks Approach" to execution: the practice of doing something that is not too easy, but not too challenging. Daniel Pink suggests that the trick to successful habit-forming behavior is to give yourself a challenge that will be attainable, yet out of your comfort zone. Pink calls this "a place of productive discomfort."[6]

Personally, I started boosting my own confidence and getting out of my quiet persona comfort zone through speaking to small groups. I shared my thoughts with my immediate team where I felt I had confidence and trust. I asked other teammates to encourage and push me to speak up. I may not be an orator, but the fear and dread I used to have about speaking engagements have definitely become a thing of the past, though I still get butterflies in my tummy before I get to the podium.

Fundamentals!

- Don't rush.
- It's about excellence, not perfection.
- The quality of practice will affect the outcome.
- Success breeds confidence.
- Don't drink from the firehose—slow your client down.
- Fall in love with monotony.
- Perform tasks repeatedly.

Make Them Sweat

- Encourage your client to step outside of their comfort zone.
- Stretch your client to the edge of their ability.

- Forget the path of least resistance. Use resistance to your advantage.
- Remember that your client may have periods when they doubt their ability and desire; revisit the Compelling Vision and emphasize FISH (Focus, Insist, Strengthen, and Hope; Part 4, p. 94).

During the execution phase you may start to see your client struggle a little more—especially if what they are doing is truly challenging. Remind them that this pain will lead to gain. Traction comes with friction. They are moving forward. Help your client navigate through the tough parts of the journey and don't allow them to give in and sabotage their growth by slipping back into their comfort zone. Show them the progress that they are making, encourage them, and offer reassurance if they exhibit doubts. Earlier, when the process was being established, you agreed that the skills you defined together were essential in achieving their vision and dream. There is no such thing as natural ability. They may well need to hear this again.

> "YOUR BELIEFS BECOME YOUR THOUGHTS, YOUR THOUGHTS BECOME YOUR WORDS, YOUR WORDS BECOME YOUR ACTIONS, YOUR ACTIONS BECOME YOUR HABITS, YOUR HABITS BECOME YOUR VALUES, YOUR VALUES BECOME YOUR DESTINY."
>
> —Mahatma Ghandi

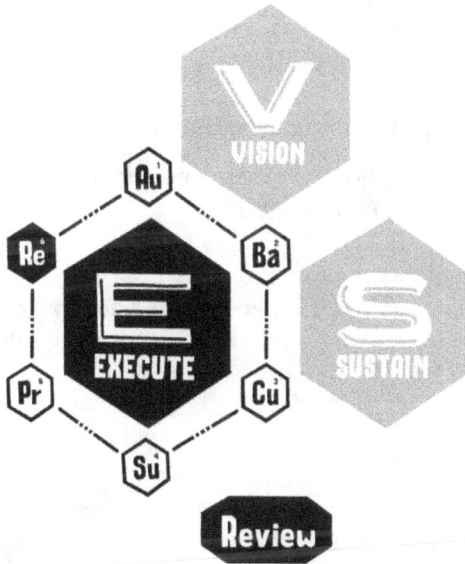

The importance of reviewing performance during the execution stage cannot be overstated. It requires constant vigilance to ensure your client makes the right habits and follows the right types of practice. The system of review can become a welcome norm once you have established a culture of coaching [Part I, p. 24] and of transparency [Part 1, p. 28]. If this hasn't been done and isn't practiced in the organization, attempts to review performance can create mistrust and divisive feelings. Dream Catcher fosters development in a high-trust environment.

It is at this juncture that you and your client must set up regular meetings for the following purposes:

- Review performance and address weak areas.
- Invite the PBA to become involved to provide support and constructive criticism.
- Encourage self-reflection through journaling, which should be a daily practice. The more your client is able to self-review their performance, the better.
- Encourage your client to ask other people on their team to critique them.

Remember my teammates Jon and Taylor? Taylor brought in her coach, Jon, to evaluate her performance in a real-world situation. You need to work with your client and dedicate a few sessions to evaluate their performance. As a coach, accept that this is your own practice as well. Bring other people into meetings to observe your performance and get immediate feedback.

Journaling Prompts During Execution

The following are prompts that you can encourage your client to use when journaling at this stage of the program:

- Today, I am looking forward to . . .
- From a personal growth perspective, I am going to accomplish . . .
- I have some challenges that I am anticipating will arise, when they do I will . . .

Hijacked by the Urgent

Often mistakenly credited to former President Dwight D. Eisenhower, the time management tool, the Eisenhower Matrix, deals with the problem: "I have two kinds of problems—the urgent and the important. The urgent are not important, and the important are never urgent." The former president did use this phrase in a 1954 speech to the Second Assembly of the World Council of Churches but credited the source as Dr. J. Roscoe Miller, president of Northwestern University.

The ability to execute tasks effectively requires one to be both organized and efficient. Dream Catcher's VES program uses a 12-week session to focus the efforts of your client on achieving set targets. It is very likely that, over such a span of time, something unexpected and urgent is going to arise that may deflect your client from their aims. The Dream Catcher journey is most likely going to be in the "important" category of life. People will typically focus on the urgent, and rightfully so. Imagine a fire starting in your building as you are engaged in something important. You would drop everything "important" and fight the fire or leave—whatever is necessary from the perspective of self-preservation.

Dream Catcher aims to achieve outcomes that lead to achieving our professional or personal goals. It is not a matter of life and death. When crises come up in life, as a rule we allow such urgencies to hijack us because there are immediate and imminent consequences in not doing so.

There are a number of urgencies that could affect your client. For example, caring or tending to a sick or ailing loved one. Such matters are typically enough to take up all of the bandwidth of any person. It is to be expected that in such situations they will become disengaged from important things such as the plan you are working on with them. This is the nature of life and is to be expected.

However, there are some people who, despite being hard-working Dream Catcher clients, struggle to delineate between the urgent and the important. They do not know how to prioritize. It is important to help such people make this distinction and overcome a tendency to focus on unimportant urgent activities. They will then be able to manage their time far more effectively in order to execute what is important in realizing their vision.

Dream Catcher asks clients to transition from "firefighting" to learning to be more in control of one's destiny. That is a great skill to have—one that will help your client to be more deliberate about everything that happens in their life, including when they actually do need to move into firefighting mode.

This intentional approach leads to your client to become aware that it is their vision, not their current circumstances or emotions that truly guides them. Their vision must inspire them to stay focused and avoid becoming distracted. Help to reinforce the idea that their actions must be congruent with their clearly defined vision and goals. Refer back to the vision, and the 12-week goal.

The Garden Route

In 2009, my younger brother Ebenezer, who lives in Cape Town, South Africa, met me in Johannesburg after I flew in from Atlanta. He had borrowed our older brother Rudolph's more reliable and comfortable car. Rudolph lived in Durban, South Africa, at the time. We drove 12 hours to Harare, Zimbabwe, and met with my mother and the rest of my siblings who live all over the world. We were getting together for a long overdue family reunion—it turned out to be such a wonderful time together. A couple of weeks later, it was time to say goodbye. Before I headed back to the United States I had ten days as a tourist in South Africa. The first order of business was to return Rudolph's vehicle to Durban and, because Ebenezer and I are very spontaneous, we decided that we would just improvise from there. The journey was marred by a six-hour standoff at the Zimbabwean side of the border because the vehicle wasn't registered to either of us. The agent didn't seem to care about the official police clearance we possessed that permitted us to take the car out of South Africa—the same document that is typically needed to return it. We finally managed to get through the border after we presented the paperwork to a different border agent who was able to make sense of the issue. The more frustrating part was how, even with legitimate paperwork, I learned that the standard at the border is no different than how official business is conducted throughout the country. I had tucked $60 USD cash underneath the police clearance to incentivize the border agent to do their job. After the frustrating delay, we continued our trek into South Africa. We stopped for the night at a rather nice Protea hotel which boasted a small but refreshing game park before making our way to Durban, where we returned the car and spent a few days with our brother. It was time to journey on to Cape Town. After many days on the road, I was ready to take a flight. It was inexpensive and short, just slightly over two hours. Ebenezer, on the contrary, wanted to continue driving. He argued that it would be worth it. Usually, when I hold a strong opinion about something I do not readily change it, but on this occasion, I went with my brother's preference.

We rented a vehicle and began the journey. After three hours, I reminded Ebenezer that we would have already landed in Cape Town by now. He chuckled and made some remark about me being a whiner. After another hour or so, I reminded him that we were still on the road. He laughed and asked me if I was going to be childish and bring it up again each hour. After he called me out for my less than positive mood, he made me aware that we were in Mthatha, home to the Nelson Mandela Museum.[7] It was then that I realized that my fixation on quickly arriving in Cape Town had clouded the last five hours of the trip and I had missed out on taking in and enjoying the experience. My attitude changed.

We made the remaining 12 hours of the journey into a two-day expedition. It was breathtaking. The most exhilarating part of the journey was the Garden Route.[8] For almost 300 miles, we drove down the winding coastline, made a stop to explore Tsitsikamma Forest, a magical place with giant trees and bright wildflowers, and drove through small towns full of hospitable people.[9] As a person who loves the outdoors, it was a remarkable journey with gorgeous scenery. As we drove one stretch, I saw humpback whales emerge from the water. The next time that I take my wife and kids to South Africa we will certainly drive the Garden Route.

> "YOU DON'T HAVE TO HIKE TO THE TOP OF A MOUNTAIN TO TAKE IN THE BEAUTY OF EACH MOMENT."
>
> —Jesse Lyn Joyner

The point of my anecdote is to stress that the journey is as important as the destination. Enjoy the scenery and take in the sights. It is imperative to enjoy the process while craving the results. Live in the moment. It is at these times that we can slow down and learn and allow ourselves to really see the beauty of the process.

SUMMARY

Authenticity:

- Awareness is vital.
- Ensure that you are attending to and engaging with what is happening.
- Keep a daily log of progress, successes, and challenges.

Bandwidth:

- New habits are difficult to make stick unless space is created to apply them.
- Challenge your client to be deliberate with their routine.
- Analyze and, if need be, alter your client's learning environment.

Curiosity:

- Be a guide to your client by not simply providing answers but helping them to discover for themselves.
- Encourage your client to be a continuous learner.
- Find out how and what your client has learned between sessions.

Support:

- Your client must share their dream with others, especially their PBA.

> ■ Help your client identify the resources they will use for account-
> ability.
>
> **Practice:**
>
> ■ Structure and consistency is vital for effective practice.
> ■ Small, attainable victories must be established for your client.
> ■ Deliberate practice is essential.
> ■ Ensure that your client stays outside of their comfort zone.
>
> **Review:**
>
> ■ Journaling is a great review tool.
> ■ Meetings with your client must encourage introspection and
> reflection.
> ■ Help your client to articulate and anticipate potential threats to
> their plan.
> ■ Remind your client that the journey is as important as their des-
> tination. They must slow down and take it all in. Avoid rushing
> and being frustrated.

Notes

1. Heidegger, M. (1996). *Being and time.* Albany: State University of New York Press.
2. Pink, D. H. (2011). *Drive: The surprising truth about what motivates us.* New York, NY: Riverhead Books.
3. Dweck, C. S. (2012). *Mindset: How you can fulfil your potential.* London, England: Constable & Robinson.
4. Sanders, C., & DeMicco, K. (Directors). (2013). *The Croods* [Motion picture]. USA: DreamWorks Animation.
5. https://www.ethos3.com/2018/01/an-analysis-of-william-h-mcravens-commencement-speech/
6. Pink, D. H. (2012). *Drive: The surprising truth about what motivates us.* New York, NY: Riverhead Books.
7. South Africa. (n.d.). Retrieved from https://www.places.co.za/html/mthatha.html
8. Lonely Planet. (n.d.). *Garden Route travel.* Retrieved from https://www.lonelyplanet.com/south-africa/the-garden-route
9. The Tsitsikamma Forest. (n.d.). Retrieved October 25, 2018, from http://country.southafrica.net/country/us/en/articles/entry/article-en-us-the-tsitsikamma-forest

12

Sustain

A luta continua, vitória é certa!
The struggle continues, victory is certain!

Dream Catcher, pages 145–149
Copyright © 2019 by Information Age Publishing

*Habit: A settled or regular tendency or practice, especially one
that is difficult to give up.*[1]

In order to attain a Compelling Vision there are particular behaviors and habits one must learn to adapt to. Most of us already have established life habits, but to follow the Dream Catcher program, it is essential to alter or, in some cases, completely give up some of these difficult-to-part-with tendencies. It is also essential to learn new habits and, in turn, make these new behaviors difficult to give up in order to Sustain!

Charles Duhigg wrote extensively about neuroscience-based studies regarding the formation of habits in his book *The Power of Habit.*[2] Duhigg noted the observations of 19th-century psychologist William James, who said, "All our life . . . is but a mass of habits." But what needs to be done in order to create positive new habits that can assist us with learning? Duhigg spent time understanding research on the brain in order to show that the prefrontal cortex is responsible for the intentional learning of new information. He elaborated on how information is then repetitively learned in a part of the brain called the basal ganglia, which transforms intentional learning into automatic behavior—habitual responses to antecedent stimuli. The MIT researchers that he cited discovered a simple neurological loop at the core of every habit. It consists of three parts:

- THE CUE: This is also known as the reminder. It can be considered to be the antecedent stimuli. It is the trigger that causes your brain to go into an automatic mode as a behavior unfolds.
- THE ROUTINE: The second part of a habit is the behavior itself. This is what most people see as the habit at face value. It is important to note that it is but one of three parts of the habit loop.
- THE REWARD: If the reward is positive, then you'll have a desire to repeat the action again. This is the final part of the habit-forming process. It provides something that the brain likes. Because the brain likes it, the pattern is remembered to be repeated in the future. The loop is complete and a habit is in formation.

The prefrontal cortex is responsible for functions including, but not limited to, complex cognitive behavior and decision-making.[3] However, as a cue becomes established and is associated with a behavior, routine, or a reward, the basal ganglia take over, thereby creating an automatic behavior.

CUE

REWARD ★ ∞ ROUTINE

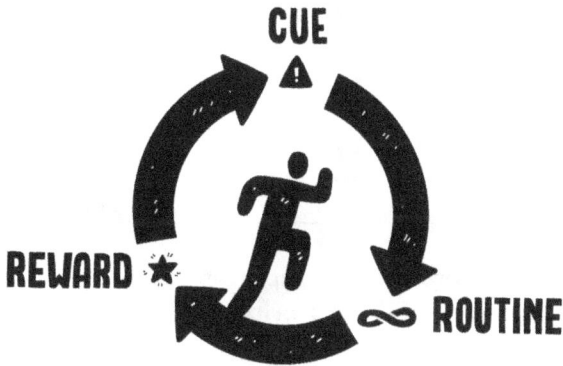

Typically, when people think of habits, they attribute them to aspects of life that are either odd or at times unhealthy. Examples of such habits include the rather innocent cookie-eating habit that Duhigg cited in his book, to more serious habits such as drug and alcohol dependency as experienced by my friend Joe. Duhigg had developed a routine of having a daily cookie. It felt good hanging out in the university cafeteria eating the cookie, yet the weight gain he experienced from this lack of self-discipline felt terrible. He wanted to break the habit and yet his attempts were ineffective. He would read a "No More Cookies" sticky note stuck to his computer as he left his desk to go the cafeteria to no avail. Eventually, he was successful. He realized that the problem with his habit was the reward aspect—the "feel-good" part. It was not the idea of eating the cookie that he felt good about, but the reward that he received—social time spent with his colleagues after long hours working on his screen. The cookie in the cafeteria was merely a part of the routine that he used as a reason to leave his desk and spend time with whichever of his associates were in the cafeteria at that particular time. Duhigg took the first step of understanding his routine and understanding the reward he was seeking. Once he did that, he was able to understand the cue.

This is crucial for a Dream Catcher coach to know. If you are going to help your client break old habits and adopt new and healthy practices and customs, it is important to help them identify the cue for unhelpful behavior. Duhigg dissected his habit into five categories: location, time of day, his emotional state, whether or not there were other people around him, and the immediate action that preceded his eating the cookie. Certain patterns became clear: a consistent time of day, his emotional state of being bored, and working alone. He was then able to devise a plan to break his cookie habit: "At 3:30 every day, I will walk to a friend's desk and talk for 10 minutes."[4]

Help your client to break their destructive habits by following Duhigg's mantra:

When I see: _____ (CUE).

I will do: _____ (ROUTINE).

In order to get: _____ (REWARD).

This same habit formation principle can also be applied to sustaining successful behavior. Dream Catcher helps clients develop practices that will help them sustain new habits and incorporate them into their everyday lives.

Take the Long View and Embrace Change

The main reason why fads fail is because they are not sustainable. Through the use of slogans and inflated and unrealistic promises of "results in 21 days," people have succumbed to marketing schemes that are simply geared to making fast money. Fads are designed to appeal to a short-acting dopamine-fueled impulse in people and thus have a very short lifecycle. As I wrote in a blog in 2016, the world had become hooked on a craze that, in my opinion, was merely a fad—Pokémon Go.[5] "In two months' time, it will be dying off, if not already extinct," I wrote then. I am by no means claiming that I can see into the future, but my prediction was true. Pokémon Go died a rather swift death.

Dream Catcher is no fad.

Dream Catcher's concept of developing a vision, then putting into action the necessary steps to achieve it through the agreement of a plan that can be successfully executed and sustained, has been outlined in this book. However, there is even more that coaches need to do to help their clients.

During my time coaching people in different businesses, I have witnessed many people develop their skills, elevate their lives, and in turn become tremendous assets to their organizations. For example, at QLI, I have had clients who have gone on to be recipients of the prestigious James P. O'Donnell Demonstrated Excellence Award. This award is given to only a very small percentage of QLI staff every other year. It is seen as being a great honor as QLI has a reputation of hiring individuals who are committed to excellence. Awardees go through a very rigorous and extensive selection process that looks for a *sustained* demonstration of excellence. These winners are seen as habitually being at the top of their game.

There is a clear foundational logic to why Dream Catcher isn't a simple check-off-move-on program. Dream Catcher's VES program is about creating a metamorphosis through careful and deliberate methods that transcend business and life silos. It doesn't promise quick results. Instead, VES ensures that participants who really apply themselves to the program will successfully develop if they remain committed.

If you doubt this fact, think back to Professor Ericsson's book *Peak* and consider his studies on mastering skills.[6] Ericsson convincingly challenged the old belief that talent is simply innate. He made a strong case that success in today's world requires a focus on practicing performance, not just on the accumulation of information. This is known as deliberate practice. The VES process enables participants to master new skills by having a crystal clear vision/dream, an accurate self-assessment of where they are today, a clear analysis of what the skill gap is and why it exists, and finally, strategies and tools for them to effectively close The Gap.

The strategies outlined in the VES process are succinct and uncomplicated. The application, however, is challenging. This is because even where there is a desire for more from life, there tends to be an aversion to one of the key by-products of growth—change!

Dream Catcher is analogous to growth. And it definitely means change. This in turn means accepting the reality of impending change in order to build habits that are transformative.

> "THE NOTION OF DEVELOP-
> MENT IS INTERCONNECTED
> TO THE CONCEPT OF CHANGE.
> THEREFORE, WHILE WE STRIVE
> TOWARDS DEVELOPMENT,
> CHANGE IS COMPULSORY."
>
> —Ebenezer Mahupete

Notes

1. Habit: Definition of habit in English by Oxford Dictionaries. (n.d.). Retrieved from https://en.oxforddictionaries.com/definition/habit
2. Duhigg, C. (2014). *The Power of habit.* New York, NY: Random House.
3. Prefrontal Cortex. (2018, September 17). Retrieved from https://www.neuro psychotherapist.com/prefrontal-cortex/
4. How Habits Work. (n.d.). Retrieved from https://charlesduhigg.com/how-habits-work/
5. Mahupete, T. (2016, July 27). *Freedom series. Part IV. The finale.* Retrieved from https://www.linkedin.com/pulse/freedom-series-part-iv-finale-tinashe-nash-mahupete/
6. Ericsson, A. (2017). *Peak: Secrets from the new science of expertise.* Boston, MA: Mariner Books.

13

Elements to Sustain

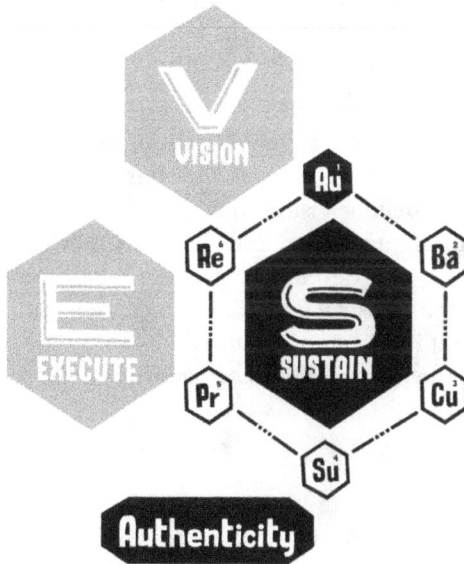

The Genuine Self is a Confident Self

Carl Rogers is a distinguished American psychologist who suggested that people have an actualizing tendency, or a need to achieve their full potential—a concept that came from Abraham Maslow's earlier work on "self-actualization."[1,2]

> "HAPPINESS IS WHEN WHAT YOU THINK, WHAT YOU SAY, AND WHAT YOU DO ARE IN HARMONY."
>
> —Mahatma Gandhi

Rogers believes that a fully functioning person is continually working toward becoming self-actualized. Such an individual has received unconditional positive regard from others, does not place conditions on his or her own worth, is capable of expressing feelings, and is fully open to life's many experiences, including upholding pro-social values. Rogers argues in favor of the importance of preserving the stability, coherence, and authenticity of our self-concept.[3] Researchers have been able to draw a correlation between Rogers' push for authenticity and the idea of maintaining passion and perseverance over a long stretch of time. Swedish researchers Mia Vainio and Daiva Daukantait refer to this state as "grit." Their research concluded that for passion and perseverance to be sustained, there needed to be a sense of authenticity as prescribed by Carl Rogers.

Research has also uncovered that, in order to sustain and persevere, a few other factors—including determination, motivation, and a sense of coherence—are also essential.[4] Dream Catcher has been modeled around these factors: A Compelling Vision that creates a sense of purpose in life, the idea of promoting autonomy for clients as they focus on mastery to pursue their dreams, and developing positive relationships with others to provide support and constructive critical feedback. Successful outcomes have been prevalent in Dream Catcher clients who have come to embrace self-acceptance as the first essential step towards personal development.

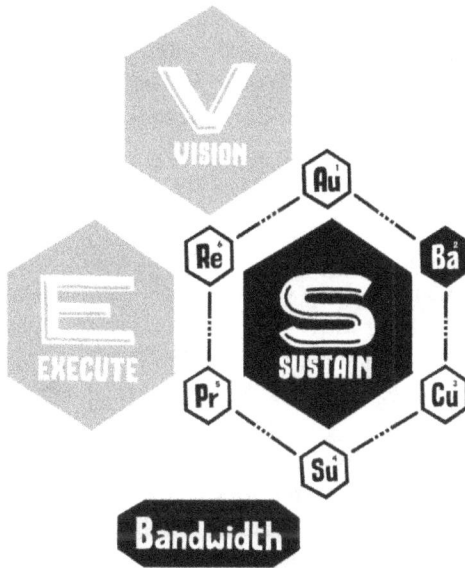

A tourist was walking with a guide through a village. As he was taking in the sights, his eyes fell upon an elephant. It was a massive and magnificent animal. He stood face to face with the majestic beast and realized that it was held by a rope around its leg. That rope was tethered to a small stake driven into the ground. Every time the elephant walked and felt the slightest tension from the rope, it would immediately stop. The tourist was horrified and asked his guide how such a powerful beast was leashed and why it couldn't simply walk away by uprooting the stake. The guide explained to him that the villagers had taken the elephant in as a baby and tied it to a tree with the very same rope. Because it is the nature of elephants to roam free, the baby elephant instinctively tried with all its might to break away, however, it wasn't yet strong enough to do so. Realizing its efforts were of no use, it finally gave up and stopped the struggle. The guide explained, "Even as a powerful adult elephant, it concedes and relents to the fact that this rope and tension has power and dominion over it."

There are times when I have coached individuals whose capacity was limited by low self-confidence. Their lives had been defined by others from their past who had told them what they could and could not be. They were much like the powerful elephant—held down by an old rope tied to a small stake. They seemed stuck. As their lives changed through becoming involved with Dream Catcher, some thrived and never looked back. A few made successful gains and then, when they felt the tug of the proverbial rope, seemed that they would revert back to their submissive selves. They needed a coach who was patient and supportive. One who would remind them how amazing they were—just as the elephant needed to be reminded of its power. As a coach, you will inspire and motivate people. That inspiration will help them in times when they question themselves.

Below are a few ideas to enthuse your client and enable them to remain on the right path.

- Send your client a note, card, text, or email telling them how proud you are of them for a specific accomplishment.
- Share something with your client that they will appreciate that chimes with their sense of curiosity. They may prefer a link to a blog, an article, or a book. Share what you know makes sense for them.
- Remember to always humanize yourself. Your story will help your client see that they aren't the only fallible being in the world—something someone may have told them that continuously echoes.
- Be enthusiastic when you connect with them; your genuine smile, positive energy, and caring concern may just be the simple thing they need.

There are others suggestions that you can access at **www.idreamidare .com**.

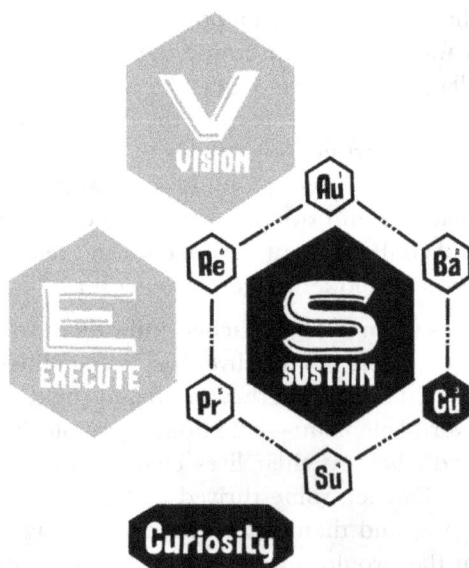

In her book *Rebel Talent*, behavioral scientist Francesca Gino shares great stories about how and when to break the rules.[5] She presents arguments in favor of nonconformists and stresses the value of being a rebel. She delved further into the topic in the NPR podcast *Hidden Brain*, hosted by Shankar Vedantam. They discussed the sensational story of the now-retired commercial airline pilot Captain Chesley Burnett Sullenberger. "Sully" became a household name after a bird strike disabled both engines of Flight 1549 just after takeoff from New York and he successfully landed the aircraft on the Hudson River, saving the lives of all 155 passengers and crew. The U.S. Airways flight from LaGuardia to Charlotte was, for a man with over 20,000 flight hours logged, theoretically a walk in the park. The "Miracle on the Hudson" has become something of a mythical act of skill and bravery. And it was. He later said that he made his decision because, after a quick analysis, it was clear to him that the only place in the highly developed New York metropolitan area that had a long enough, wide enough, and smooth enough area to land on was the river. Sully wasn't merely following the script or what he'd learned in his training. He remained open-minded. All within the 208 seconds he had to make a life-or-death decision.

Gino explained that one of the things that many people might not know about Sully was that he had served as a volunteer on teams that looked at prior air accidents and tried to understand what had happened. He had a lot of experience when he found himself in that dire situation. Not only had he prepared for that particular day, he also followed a unique routine. Any time he walked onto a plane he asked himself, "What is it that I can learn. How can this be different?" As experienced as he was, he had the kind of intellectual humility and curiosity in how things could be different that kept him open-minded. That is what saved those lives. If you aren't continually learning, you're obsolete! Not just obsolete—sometimes a figurative (in Sully's case, literal) danger to others.

Make sure that your client is—or becomes—a lifelong learner, open to new ways of doing things.

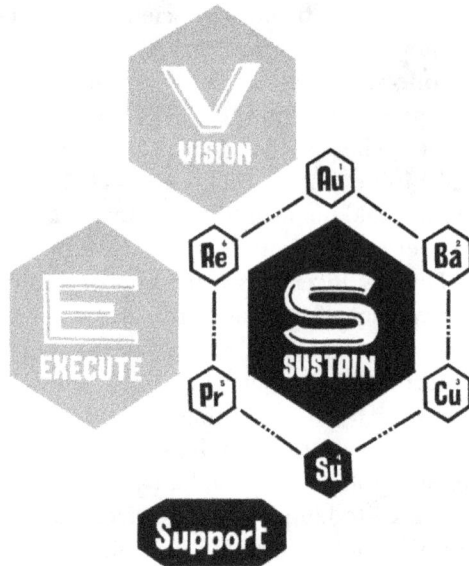

Share the Dream

The Compelling Vision—the dream—distills all of the great things your client wants out of life over the next three years. As clients share their dream with others, the simple act of speaking about their commitment to change serves as an affirmation that helps clients believe in themselves. What you say of yourself, you become!

Sharing the dream also helps your client to develop a deeper sense of ownership of and accountability for the work that needs to be done. When they have committed to what their compass and path in life is meant to be, they begin to become responsible for their own self.

Dream sharing garners support both from their PBA (Personal Board Advisors) and others also taking the Dream Catcher program. The latter group will support each other and call each other out if someone is deviating from their Compelling Vision.

PBA Meetings

What good is a PBA if you do not spend time with its members? Your client must schedule time to spend with those they have recruited to support them. Remind your client that, in this phase, they need to be strategic with this practice. Time is a valuable resource and the individuals recruited to a

PBA are likely to have little of it to spare. Ensure that your client has a clear plan and agenda for meeting with their PBA. Of course, some advisors may be happy with a more organic and casual approach, but your client must approach each advisor in the way that suits them.

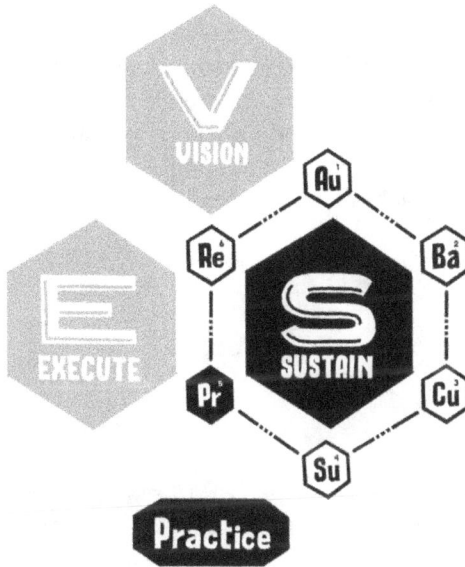

Don't Break the Chain

Brad Isaac is a software developer with an interesting history.[6] Before he went into the world of IT, he toured as a stand-up comic performing on stages with people like Norm MacDonald and Carrot Top and briefly wrote for *The Tonight Show with Jay Leno*. Around this time, he found himself at a comedy club asking Jerry Seinfeld for advice. Brad described the interaction.[7]

Seinfeld told him that to be a better comic he had to write better jokes and the way to do that was to write every day—even when you don't feel like it!

He advised Brad to get a big wall calendar setting out the entire year on a single page and then to hang it on a prominent wall in his living space. Next, he would need a big red permanent marker. For each day that Brad completed his task of writing, he would get to put a big red X on that day. Jerry elaborated, "After a few days you'll have a chain. Just keep at it and the chain will grow longer every day. You'll like seeing that chain, especially when you get a few weeks under your belt. Your only job is to not break the chain."

Seinfeld's emphasis wasn't about the quality of the material that he wrote. Instead, the focus was on creating a habit—on "not breaking the chain."

Brad has taken this advice into his other ventures and it has proven to be successful. Dream Catcher has produced success using the same approach with all of its clients. Some have used an actual calendar to create the chain. Others have capitalized on technology and created a reminder and accountability system on **www.idreamidare.com** that helps create a chain for the plans coaches use with their clients.

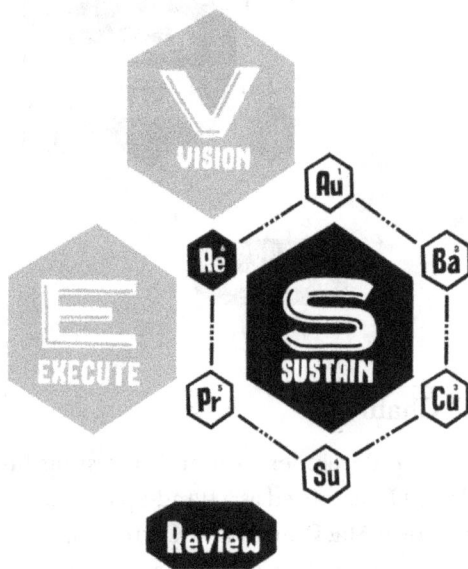

Demystifying Privacy

Your client's mental hijacks will appear when emotion overrides rationale and reasoning. New habits are often very fragile, and it is for this reason that you and your client should be aware of and deal with any issue that may deter the Compelling Vision from becoming a sustained reality. As people, there are moments when we are all likely to want to leave the field, especially when we drop the ball. "It's not worth it," we tell ourselves. "I can never be the leader I dream to be." It is imperative to recognize that these attitudes are likely the same things that have tripped your client up in the past. Whatever the previous hurdles were, they are likely to reappear. This is why your client should share their vision. Involving others who understand what those previous hurdles might have been can be the backstop strategy when things aren't going to plan.

When I first followed the process of doing my Review (journaling, asking others to critique me), I found it discomforting. As I've said, I'm a private person. However, as I continued, I not only became more comfortable, I saw great benefits from the process. I realized that sharing helped me create a better bond with people that I had not previously been close to. It also seemed to help those around me that found the challenges that I was facing relatable. The process of reviewing how I am doing has taught me how to think about what happens in my life in a way that makes sense. Learning to share has also helped me accept and be more at ease, more at peace with the thoughts I typically used to hide and avoid. It has especially helped me reaffirm my values and Compelling Vision with pride.

Dream Catcher coaches and clients have expressed the same sentiment. When they have broken the barrier of privacy, they have been able to organically enlist people able to review their performance, leading to sustained success.

Review the Compelling Vision

The VES (Vision, Execute, Sustain) process now requires the coach to review the Compelling Vision with their client. Because Dream Catcher's philosophy emphasizes independence, it is important that the client initiates this process. This review is going to benefit your client as they apply newly learned habits to the next 12-week session and also to other aspects of their life. If they desire to amend their Compelling Vision at this point—and, hopefully, after being able to witness their growth and see further ahead with greater clarity, they *will*—you should revisit the process described in Chapter 7 and rerun the process on "How to create a vision." Once this is done, you will review it with them as you have done in the past. This is likely to be a very inspiring process, as you see how energized your client has become by learning how to dream bigger and more vividly. After the initial 12-week session is completed, you will repeat the process by focusing on a new area for development over the next 12 weeks.

SUMMARY

Sustain the learning and *skill building* process.

Promote positive habits for learning and self-development.

Use the habit creation loop to identify the cue and reward to help establish a positive routine.

Get rid of bad habits that sabotage skill development.

Take the long view. This is not a fad.

Authenticity:

- Actualization leads to your client fulfilling their potential.
- Determination, motivation, and a sense of coherence lead to success.

Bandwidth:

- What previous beliefs from the past does your client need to be emancipated from?
- Check that your client has the necessary confidence to sustain their progress and, if necessary, boost it by taking positive action.

Curiosity:

- Encourage your client to be open minded and receptive to new ways of seeing and doing things.
- Share essential resources with your client.
- Ask your client to use journaling to highlight new learning.

Support:

- Ask your client to share their dream with others, either in their PBA or with colleagues following the Dream Catcher program.
- Encourage your client to meet with their PBA.

Practice:

- Don't break the chain. Support your client in building and sustaining new and positive habits.
- Use visual aids to embed habit formation.

Review:

- Ask your client to share the dream with others to get supportive feedback and demystify privacy.
- Continue the practice of journaling.
- Ask your client to independently review and edit their Compelling Vision.

You are done with the first 12-week session. Your client has learned the art of mastering new skills, closing The Gap, and has taken steps towards making their ever-developing Compelling Vision a reality. Dream Catcher has stretched you as a coach as well. You are now ready to repeat the process as you set up another 12-week session using the process we have outlined. Utilize all of the Dream Catcher principles you have learned and trust yourself as a coach. The VES process is challenging and rigorous and has required you to be creative and flexible. As you commit to your own growth, you will continue to improve and make the process your modality, both with other clients and in your life.

I encourage both coaches and clients to take some time to appreciate not only the knowledge they now have of the program, but also the skills that they have acquired by following it.

Notes

1. Rogers, C. R. (2004). *On becoming a person: A therapist's view of psychotherapy.* London, England: Constable.
2. Maslow, A. H. (2011). Hierarchy of needs: A theory of human motivation. https://www.all-about-psychology.com
3. Vainio, M. M., & Daukantait, D. (2015). Grit and different aspects of well-being: Direct and indirect relationships via sense of coherence and authenticity. *Journal of Happiness Studies,17*(5), 2119–2147.
4. Olsson, M., Hansson, K., Lundblad, A., & Cederblad, M. (2006). Sense of coherence: Definition and explanation. *International Journal of Social Welfare, 15*(3), 219–229.
5. Gino, F. (2018). Rebel talent: Why it pays to break the rules at work and in life. New York, NY: Dey St., an imprint of William Morrow.
6. About. (n.d.). Retrieved September 14, 2018, from http://persistenceunlimited.com/about/
7. Trapani, G. (2013, June 25). Brad Isaacs "Jerry Seinfeld's productivity secret." Retrieved from https://lifehacker.com/281626/jerry-seinfelds-productivity-secret

14

Conclusion

It never ends!

The Dream Catcher coaching program is a way of life, an ethos, a code of conduct, and a commitment. By applying the concepts outlined in the book you will see the amazing results that Dream Catcher produces for coaches, clients, and ultimately, their businesses and communities.

It is a great shame that many businesses fail to take the road less travelled and invest in their future success by placing just a little bit of time, energy, and effort into developing their team members. The plague of disengaged employees can and must end. Most businesses agree that there is a problem and are searching for solutions that can help with the underlying issues. Sadly, many of the solutions businesses utilize are ineffective. To create loyalty and engagement from team members, higher pay, bonuses, "fun days," and other ludicrous incentives are offered. The truth is that you cannot buy loyalty and engagement; it has to be earned. Dream Catcher is the solution to earning that loyalty. Empower your team members and they will invest in the mission and success of your organization.

Dream Catcher, pages 163–164
Copyright © 2019 by Information Age Publishing
All rights of reproduction in any form reserved.

It is my belief that if a solution is only applicable to business, and not to other parts of our lives, then it is flawed. Dream Catcher's methods, its Elements, and the VES (Visions, Execute, Sustain) model have shown that they are not only effective in the workplace but are also pertinent to our communities and our home lives. I have been excited to see Dream Catcher methods applied in different businesses, sectors, and industries around the United States. As I have shared the concepts with other people internationally there has been amazing feedback from those who see great possibilities in the Dream Catcher credo.

Close your eyes.

Imagine.

Dream about your business and visualize your team members. They are competent, engaged, and invested in your company. They are excited to grow, have a thirst to learn more about the company and are completely committed to your mission.

Open your eyes!

All of this can happen when you open your eyes and your mind.

Enjoy the process of developing the people around you. May they dream vividly, may they dare greatly, and may they do amazing things with their lives!

Dream. Dare. Do!